red hot
gourmet

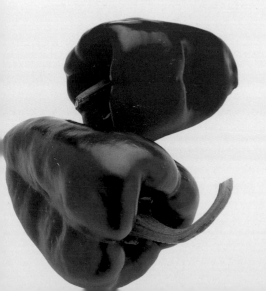

red hot

Published by:
TRIDENT PRESS INTERNATIONAL
801 12th Avenue South
Suite 302
Naples, FL 34102 U.S.A.
(c)Trident Press
Tel: (941) 649 7077
Fax: (941) 649 5832
Email: tridentpress@worldnet.att.net
Website: www.trident-international.com

Red Hot Gourmet
Packaged by R&R Publications
Marketing Pty Ltd
Design and Production: Icon Partners
Food Photography: William Meppem
Food Stylists: Donna Hay
Assistant: Angela Nahas

Recipe Development: Donna Hay, Angela Nahas
Proof Reader: Samantha Calcott
Includes Index
ISBN 1 582 791155
EAN 9 781582 791159

First Edition Printed September 2000
Computer Typeset in
& Times New Roman
Printed by APP Printing, Singapore
Film Scanning by PICA Overseas, Singapore

CONTENTS

Tastes of Thailand

Snacks and Starters	4
Soups	6
Salads	8
Stir-Fries	10
Curry	20
Steamed Grilled & Fried	28
Noodles & Rice Dishes	34

Flavours of Mexico

Starters, Soups & Snacks	37
Fish & Seafood	50
Meat & Poultry	58
Salads and Vegetables	66
Sauces and Condiments	73
Glossary	75

gourmet

Snacks and Starters

▶ *Coconut milk and coconut cream are essentially the same product. Coconut cream is very thick coconut milk and is the result of the first pressing of the coconut flesh. Coconut milk and cream can be purchased in various forms or you can make them yourself.*

RICE CAKES
with LIME CRAB

2 cups/440 g/14 oz jasmine rice, cooked
30 g/1 oz coriander (cilantro) leaves, chopped
crushed black peppercorns
vegetable oil for deep-frying

LIME CRAB TOPPING
185g/6oz canned crab meat, well-drained
2 fresh red chillies, seeded and chopped
2 small fresh green chillies, finely sliced
¹/₄ cup/60 mL/2 fl oz coconut cream
2 tablespoons thick natural yogurt
3 teaspoons lime juice
3 teaspoons Thai fish sauce (nam pla)
3 teaspoons finely grated lime rind
1 tablespoon crushed black peppercorns

1 Combine rice, coriander (cilantro) and black peppercorns to taste, then press into an oiled 18 x 28 cm/7 x 11 in shallow cake tin and refrigerate until set. Cut rice mixture into 3 x 4 cm/1¹/₄ x 1¹/₂ in rectangles.

2 Heat vegetable oil in a large saucepan until a cube of bread dropped in browns in 50 seconds and cook rice cakes, a few at a time, for 3 minutes or until golden. Drain on absorbent kitchen paper.

3 To make topping, place crab meat, red and green chillies, coconut cream, yogurt, lime juice and fish sauce in a food processor and process until smooth. Stir in lime rind and black peppercorns. Serve with warm rice cakes. **Makes 24**

FISH CAKES
with RELISH

500 g/1 lb boneless fine fleshed fish fillets
3 tablespoons Thai red curry paste
2 tablespoons chopped coriander (cilantro) leaves
1 tablespoon fresh basil leaves
1 egg white
90 g/3 oz green beans, finely chopped
2 kaffir lime leaves, finely shredded (optional)
vegetable oil for shallow-frying

CUCUMBER RELISH
1 cucumber, seeded and chopped
1 fresh red chilli, chopped
1 tablespoon sugar
2 tablespoons rice vinegar
1 tablespoon water
1 tablespoon chopped roasted peanuts (optional)

1 Place fish, curry paste, coriander (cilantro), basil and egg white in a food processor and process to make a smooth thick paste. Place mixture in a bowl, add beans and lime leaves (if using) and mix to combine. Cover and refrigerate for 1 hour.

2 To make relish, place cucumber, chilli, sugar, vinegar, water and peanuts (if using) in a bowl and mix to combine. Cover and refrigerate until required.

3 Using wet or lightly oiled hands, take 2 tablespoons of fish mixture and roll into a ball, then flatten to form a disk. Repeat with remaining fish mixture.

4 Heat about 2.5 cm/1 in oil in a frying pan over a high heat and cook fish cakes, a few at a time, for 2 minutes each side or until well browned and cooked through. Drain on absorbent kitchen paper and serve hot fish cakes with relish. **Makes 12-14**

Rice vinegar is made from fermented rice and generally it is milder than Western vinegars. If unavailable, diluted white or cider vinegar can be used instead.

FISH CAKES WITH RELISH

▶ *Straw mushrooms are one of the most popular mushrooms used in Asian cooking and in the West are readily available canned. Oyster mushrooms are also known as abalone mushrooms and range in colour from white to grey to pale pink. Their shape is similar to that of an oyster shell and they have a delicate flavour. Oyster mushrooms should not be eaten raw as some people are allergic to them in the uncooked state.*

HOT *and* SOUR SEAFOOD SOUP

4 red or golden shallots, sliced
2 fresh green chillies, chopped
6 kaffir lime leaves
4 slices fresh ginger
8 cups/2 litres/3¹/₂ pt fish, chicken
or vegetable stock
250 g/8 oz boneless firm fish fillets,
cut into chunks
12 medium uncooked prawns, shelled
and deveined
12 mussels (or clams), scrubbed and beards
removed
125 g /4 oz oyster or straw mushrooms
3 tablespoons lime juice
2 tablespoons Thai fish sauce (nam pla)
fresh coriander leaves
lime wedges

1 Place shallots, chillies, lime leaves, ginger and stock in a saucepan and bring to the boil over a high heat. Reduce heat and simmer for 3 minutes.

2 Add fish, prawns, mussels (clams) and mushrooms and cook for 3-5 minutes or until fish and seafood are cooked, discard any mussels that do not open after 5 minutes cooking. Stir in lime juice and fish sauce. To serve, ladle soup into bowls, scatter with coriander (cilantro) leaves and accompany with lime wedges. **Serves 6**

CHILLI KUMARA

CHILLI KUMARA SOUP

6 cups/1.5 litres/2¹/₂ pt chicken stock
3 stalks fresh lemon grass, bruised, or 1¹/₂ teaspoons dried lemon grass, soaked in hot water until soft
3 fresh red chillies, halved
10 slices fresh or bottled galangal or fresh ginger
5-6 fresh coriander (cilantro)plants, roots washed,
leaves removed and reserved
1 large kumara (orange sweet potato), peeled and cut into 2 cm/3/4 in pieces
3/4 cup/185 ml/6 fl oz coconut cream
1 tablespoon Thai fish sauce (nam pla)

1   Place stock, lemon grass, chillies, galangal or ginger and coriander (cilantro) roots in a saucepan and bring to the boil over a medium heat. Add kumara (sweet potato) and simmer, uncovered, for 15 minutes or until kumara (sweet potato) is soft.

2 Remove lemon grass, galangal or ginger and coriander (cilantro) roots and discard. Cool liquid slightly, then purée soup, in batches, in a food processor or blender. Return soup toa clean saucepan and stir in ¹/₂ cup/125 mL/4 fl oz of the coconut cream and the fish sauce. Cook, stirring, over a medium heat for4 minutes or until heated. Stir in two-thirdsof the reserved coriander (cilantro) leaves.

3 To serve, ladle soup into bowls, top with a little of the remaining coconut cream and scatter with remaining coriander (cilantro) leaves. **Serves 4**

Coriander is used extensively in Thai cooking and it is one of the ingredients that gives Thai food its distinctive flavour. Fresh coriander is readily available from greengrocers and is usually sold as the whole plant.

THAI
BEEF SALAD

THAI BEEF SALAD

500 g/1 lb rump or topside steak
185 g/6 oz mixed lettuce leaves
185 g/6 oz cherry tomatoes, halved
2 cucumbers, peeled and chopped
2 red onions, sliced
3 tablespoons fresh mint leaves

LIME AND CORIANDER DRESSING

1 stalk fresh lemon grass, chopped or
1 teaspoon finely grated lemon rind
3 tablespoons fresh coriander (cilantro) leaves
1 tablespoon brown sugar
2 tablespoons lime juice
3 tablespoons light soy sauce

2 tablespoons sweet chilli sauce
2 teaspoons Thai fish sauce (nam pla)

1 Heat a frying or char-grill pan over a high heat until hot, add beef and cook for 1-2 minutes each side or until cooked to your liking. Set aside to cool.

2 Arrange lettuce, tomatoes, cucumbers, onions and mint attractively on a serving platter.

3 To make dressing, place lemon grass or rind, coriander (cilantro), sugar, lime juice and soy, chilli and fish sauces in a bowl and mix to combine.

4 Slice beef thinly and arrange on salad, then drizzle with dressing and serve. **Serves 4**

When making a Thai salad, presentation is all important and a salad can be a spectacular centrepiece for any table. Traditionally Thai salads are served on flat plates – not in bowls – which means the full effect of the arrangement of ingredients can be appreciated.

► *To clean squid (calamari), pull tentacles from the squid (calamari), carefully taking with them the stomach and ink bag. Next cut the beak, stomach and ink bag from the tentacles and discard. Wash tentacles well. Wash 'hood' and peel away skin. For this recipe, the hoods are left whole, if you wish the tentacles can be cut into small pieces and also used.*

BARBECUED SQUID SALAD

1 tablespoon chilli oil
1 tablespoon finely grated lemon rind
2 teaspoons crushed black peppercorns
500 g/1 lb small squid (calamari) hoods, cleaned
30 g/1 oz fresh basil leaves
30 g/1 oz fresh mint leaves
30 g/1 oz fresh coriander (cilantro) leaves

LEMON AND CHILLI DRESSING
1 fresh green chilli, chopped
2 tablespoons brown sugar
3 tablespoons lemon juice
2 tablespoons light soy sauce

1 Place oil, lemon rind and peppercorns in a shallow dish and mix to combine. Add squid (calamari) and marinate for 30 minutes.

2 Line a serving platter with the basil, mint and coriander (cilantro). Cover with plastic food wrap and refrigerate until ready to serve.

3 To make dressing, place chilli, sugar, lemon juice and soy sauce in a bowl and mix to combine.

4 Preheat a barbecue, char-grill pan or frying pan and cook squid (calamari) for 30 seconds each side or until tender — take care not to overcook or the squid (calamari) will become tough. Place squid (calamari) on top of herbs and drizzle with dressing.
Serves 4

CHICKEN *with* CHILLI JAM

2 teaspoons vegetable oil
3 chicken breast fillets or 4 boneless thigh
fillets, cut into thin strips
4 red or golden shallots, chopped
185 g/6 oz broccoli, chopped
125 g/4 oz snow peas (mangetout), halved
60 g/2 oz unsalted, roasted cashews
2 tablespoons light soy sauce

CHILLI JAM
2 teaspoons vegetable oil
4 fresh red chillies, sliced
1 tablespoon shredded fresh ginger
1 teaspoon shrimp paste
1/3 cup/90 g/3 oz sugar
1/3 cup/90 mL/3 fl oz water
2 tablespoons lime juice

1 To make jam, heat oil in a wok over a
medium heat, add chillies, ginger and shrimp
paste and stir-fry for 1 minute or until golden.
Stir in sugar, water and lime juice and cook,
stirring, for 3 minutes or until mixture is thick.
Remove jam from wok and set aside.

2 Heat oil in a clean wok over a high heat
for 1 minute, add chicken and shallots and
stir-fry for 3 minutes or until chicken is
lightly browned.

3 Add broccoli, snow peas (mangetout),
cashews and soy sauce and stir-fry for
3 minutes longer or until vegetables
change colour and are cooked.

4 To serve, place chicken on serving plate
and top with Chilli Jam. **Serves 4**

*Serve this tasty chicken dish with steamed jasmine
rice. If you prefer, the Chilli Jam can be served
separately so that each diner can season their
serving according to individual taste.*

CHICKEN WITH CHILLI JAM

BEEF *with* PEPPERCORNS

2 teaspoons vegetable oil
2 cloves garlic, minced
1 fresh green chilli, chopped
500 g/1 lb topside or round steak, sliced
1 tablespoon green peppercorns in brine,
drained and lightly crushed
1 green pepper, chopped

3 tablespoons fresh coriander (cilantro) leaves
1/3 cup/90 mL/3 fl oz coconut milk
2 teaspoons Thai fish sauce (nam pla)

1 Heat oil in a wok over a high heat.
   Add garlic and chilli and cook for 1 minute.
   Add beef and peppercorns and stir-fry
   for 3 minutes or until beef is browned.

2 Stir in green pepper, coriander (cilantro),
   coconut milk and fish sauce and cook for 2
   minutes longer. **Serves 4**

*Black peppercorns are a traditional Thai ingredient and before the introduction of chillies by the Portuguese,
they were used to add heat to dishes. This spicy stir-fry teams milder green peppercorns with chilli to make the
most of two favourite ingredients*

COCONUT PRAWNS *and* SCALLOPS

1 kg/2 lb large uncooked prawns, shelled
and deveined, tails left intact
3 egg whites, lightly beaten
90 g/3 oz shredded coconut
vegetable oil for deep-frying
1 tablespoon peanut oil
4 fresh red chillies, seeded and sliced
2 small fresh green chillies, seeded and sliced
2 cloves garlic, crushed
1 tablespoon shredded fresh ginger
3 kaffir lime leaves, finely shredded
375 g/12 oz scallops
125 g/4 oz snow pea (mangetout) leaves
or sprouts
2 tablespoons palm or brown sugar

¹/₄ cup/60 mL/2 fl oz lime juice
2 tablespoons Thai fish sauce (nam pla)

1 Dip prawns in egg whites, then roll in coconut to coat. Heat vegetable oil in a large saucepan until a cube of bread dropped in browns in 50 seconds and cook prawns, a few at a time, for 2-3 minutes or until golden and crisp. Drain on absorbent kitchen paper and keep warm.

2 Heat peanut oil in a wok over a high heat, add red and green chillies, garlic, ginger and lime leaves and stir-fry for 2-3 minutes or until fragrant.

3 Add scallops to wok and stir-fry for 3 minutes or until opaque. Add cooked prawns, snow pea (mangetout) leaves or sprouts, sugar, lime juice and fish sauce and stir-fry for 2 minutes or until heated. **Serves 6**

If snow pea (mangetout) leaves or sprouts are unavailable watercress is a good alternative for this dish.

STIR-FRIED DUCK
WITH GREENS

▶ *Chinese broccoli (gai lum) is a popular Asian vegetable. It has dark green leaves on firm stalks often with small white flowers. The leaves, stalks and flowers are all used in cooking, however the stalks are considered to be the choicest part of the plant. To prepare, remove leaves from stalks and peel, then chop both leaves and stalks and use as directed in the recipe.*

STIR-FRIED DUCK *with* GREENS

1.2 kg/2½ lb Chinese barbecued
or roasted duck
2 teaspoons vegetable oil
1 tablespoon Thai red curry paste
1 teaspoon shrimp paste
1 stalk fresh lemon grass, finely sliced,
or ½ teaspoon dried lemon grass, soaked
in hot water until soft
4 fresh red chillies
1 bunch Chinese broccoli (gai lum)
or Swiss chard, chopped

1 tablespoon palm or brown sugar
2 tablespoons tamarind concentrate
1 tablespoon Thai fish sauce (nam pla)

1 Slice meat from duck, leaving the skin on, and cut into bite-sized pieces. Reserve as many of the cavity juices as possible.

2 Heat oil in a wok over a medium heat, add curry paste, shrimp paste, lemon grass and chillies and stir-fry for 3 minutes or until fragrant.

3 Add duck and reserved juices and stir-fry for 2 minutes or until coated in spice mixture and heated. Add broccoli or chard, sugar, tamarind and fish sauce and stir-fry for 3-4 minutes or until broccoli is wilted. **Serves 4**

► *Spoons and forks are used in Thailand for eating, not chopsticks. Like us, Thais would only use chopsticks when eating Chinese food.*

PORK *and* PUMPKIN STIR-FRY

2 tablespoons Thai red curry paste
2 onions, cut into thin wedges,
layers separated
2 teaspoons vegetable oil
500 g/1 lb lean pork strips
500 g/1 lb peeled butternut pumpkin (squash),
cut into 2 cm/3/4 in cubes
4 kaffir lime leaves, shredded
1 tablespoon palm or brown sugar
2 cups/500 ml/16 fl oz coconut milk
1 tablespoon Thai fish sauce (nam pla)

1 Place curry paste in wok and cook, stirring, over a high heat for 2 minutes or until fragrant. Add onions and cook for 2 minutes longer or until onions are soft. Remove from pan and set aside.

2 Heat oil in wok, add pork and stir-fry for 3 minutes or until brown. Remove pork from pan and set aside.

3 Add pumpkin, lime leaves, sugar, coconut milk and fish sauce to pan, bring to simmering and simmer for 2 minutes. Stir in curry paste mixture and simmer for 5 minutes longer. Return pork to pan and cook for 2 minutes or until heated. **Serves 4**

PORK *with* GARLIC *and* PEPPER

2 teaspoons vegetable oil
4 cloves garlic, sliced
1 tablespoon crushed black peppercorns
500 g/1 lb lean pork strips
1 bunch/500 g/1 lb baby bok choy (Chinese greens), chopped
4 tablespoons fresh coriander (cilantro) leaves
2 tablespoons palm or brown sugar
2 tablespoons light soy sauce
2 tablespoons lime juice

1 Heat oil in a wok or frying pan over a medium heat, add garlic and black peppercorns and stir-fry for 1 minute. Add pork and stir-fry for 3 minutes or until brown.

2 Add bok choy (Chinese greens), coriander, sugar, soy sauce and lime juice and stir-fry for 3-4 minutes or until pork and bok choy are tender. **Serves 4**

Bok choy is also known as Chinese chard, buck choy and pak choi. It varies in length from 10-30 cm/4-12 in. For this recipe the smaller variety is used. It has a mild, cabbage-like flavour. Ordinary cabbage could be used for this recipe.

PORK WITH GARLIC

AND PEPPER

STIR-FRIED BITTER MELON

1 medium bitter melon (gourd), peeled, seeds removed, cut into
1 cm/¹/₂ in thick slices
2 tablespoons salt
1 tablespoon vegetable oil
3 tablespoons small dried prawns
6 red or golden shallots, sliced
2 cloves garlic, sliced
2 stalks fresh lemon grass, finely sliced,
or 1 teaspoon finely grated lemon rind
3 fresh green chillies, finely sliced
1 small red pawpaw, cut into
3 cm/1¹/₄ in cubes
125 g/4 oz snow peas (mangetout), halved
1 tablespoon tamarind concentrate

1 Rub each slice of bitter melon (gourd) with salt, place in a colander and set aside for 30 minutes. Rinse under cold water and drain thoroughly.

2 Heat oil in a wok over a medium heat, add dried prawns, shallots, garlic and lemon grass or rind and stir-fry for 4 minutes or until shallots are golden.

3 Add chillies and bitter melon (gourd) and stir-fry for 4 minutes or until melon is tender. Add pawpaw, snow peas (mangetout) and tamarind and stir-fry for 2 minutes or until snow peas (mangetout) are tender. **Serves 4**

This dish is delicious served on a bed of cellophane noodles and topped with fried onions.
Bitter melon (gourd) looks somewhat like a cucumber with a lumpy skin and as the name suggests has a bitter taste. It should always be degorged with salt before using.

Stir-frying is a very quick cooking process – this dish takes less than 10 minutes – it is therefore very important that all preparation such as cutting and chopping have been completed before the cooking starts.

EGGPLANT *and* BASIL STIR-FRY

3 eggplant (aubergines), halved lengthways
and cut into 1 cm/¹/₂ in thick slices
salt
1 tablespoon vegetable oil
2 onions, cut into thin wedges,
layers separated
3 fresh red chillies, chopped
2 cloves garlic, sliced
1 stalk fresh lemon grass, chopped,
or ¹/₂ teaspoon dried lemon grass, soaked
in hot water until soft

250 g/8 oz green beans, trimmed
1 cup/250 mL/8 fl oz coconut cream
45 g/1¹/₂ oz basil leaves

1 Place eggplant (aubergines) in a colander, sprinkle with salt and set aside for 20 minutes. Rinse under cold running water and pat dry on absorbent kitchen paper.

2 Heat oil in a wok or frying pan over a high heat, add onions, chillies, garlic and lemon grass and stir-fry for 3 minutes. Add eggplant (aubergines), beans and coconut cream and stir-fry for 5 minutes or until eggplant (aubergines) are tender. Stir in basil.

Serves 6

EGGPLANT AND BASIL STIR-FRY

STIR-FRIED TAMARIND
PRAWNS

► *Tamarind is the large pod of the tamarind or Indian date tree. After picking, it is seeded and peeled, then pressed into a dark brown pulp. It is also available as a concentrate. Tamarind pulp or concentrate can be purchased from Indian food stores. In Oriental cooking it is used as a souring agent, if unavailable a mixture of lime or lemon juice and treacle can be used instead.*

STIR-FRIED
TAMARIND PRAWNS

2 tablespoons tamarind pulp
¹/₂ cup/125 ml/4 fl oz water
2 teaspoons vegetable oil
3 stalks fresh lemon grass, chopped, or
2 teaspoons finely grated lemon rind
2 fresh red chillies, chopped

**500 g/1 lb medium uncooked prawns,
shelled and deveined, tails intact**
**2 green (unripe) mangoes, peeled
and thinly sliced**
**3 tablespoons chopped fresh coriander (cilantro)
leaves**
2 tablespoons brown sugar
2 tablespoons lime juice

1 Place tamarind pulp and water in a bowl and stand for 20 minutes. Strain, reserve liquid and set aside. Discard solids.

2 Heat oil in a wok or frying pan over a high heat, add lemon grass or rind and chillies and stir-fry for 1 minute. Add prawns and stir-fry for 2 minutes or until they change colour.

3 Add mangoes, coriander, sugar, lime juice and tamarind liquid and stir-fry for 5 minutes or until prawns are cooked. **Serves 4**

MUSSELS *with* COCONUT VINEGAR

1.5 kg/3 lb mussels (clams) in their shells
6 whole coriander (cilantro) plants, washed
and roughly chopped
3 stalks fresh lemon grass, bruised,
or 1½ teaspoons dried lemon grass, soaked
in hot water until soft
5 cm/2 in piece fresh ginger, shredded
½ cup/125 ml/4 fl oz water
1 tablespoon vegetable oil
1 red onion, halved and sliced
2 fresh red chillies, sliced
2 tablespoons coconut vinegar
fresh coriander (cilantro) leaves

1 Place mussels, coriander (cilantro), lemon grass, ginger and water in a wok over a high heat. Cover and cook for 5 minutes or until mussels open. Discard any mussels that do not open after 5 minutes cooking. Remove mussels from wok, discard coriander (cilantro), lemon grass and ginger. Strain cooking liquid and reserve.

2 Heat oil in a wok over a medium heat, add onion and chillies and stir-fry for 3 minutes or until onion is soft. Add mussels, reserved cooking liquid and coconut vinegar and stir-fry for 2 minutes or until mussels are heated. Scatter with coriander leaves and serve.

Serves 4

This dish is delicious served with boiled egg noodles and topped with coriander leaves and wok juices. Coconut vinegar is made from the sap of the coconut palm. It is available from Oriental food shops. If unavailable any mild vinegar can be used instead.

CARDAMOM *and* ORANGE DUCK

1.5 kg/3 lb Chinese barbecued or roasted duck
3 cups/750 ml/1¼ pt chicken stock
2 small fresh red chillies, halved
3 cm/1¼ in piece fresh galangal or ginger, sliced, or 5 slices bottled galangal
2 stalks fresh lemon grass, cut into
3 cm/1¼ in pieces, bruised, or
1 teaspoon dried lemon grass, soaked in hot water until soft
6 whole coriander (cilantro) plants, washed, stems and roots removed, leaves reserved
6 cardamom pods, crushed
4 kaffir lime leaves, torn into pieces
1 large orange, peeled, all white pith removed from rind, flesh segmented and reserved
1 tablespoon vegetable oil
2 teaspoons shrimp paste
2 teaspoons Thai red curry paste
1 clove garlic, finely chopped
1 tablespoon palm or brown sugar
2 spring onions, cut into thin strips

1 Remove meat from duck and cut into bite-sized pieces – reserve bones, skin and as many of the juices as possible. Place reserved bones, skin and juices, stock, chillies, galangal or ginger, lemon grass, coriander (cilantro) stems and roots, cardamom pods, lime leaves and orange rind in a saucepan and bring to the boil. Reduce heat and simmer, uncovered, for 15 minutes. Strain liquid and set aside. Discard solids.

2 Heat oil in a wok or large saucepan over a medium heat, add shrimp and curry pastes and garlic and cook, stirring, for 1-2 minutes or until fragrant.

3 Add duck pieces and stir to coat with spice paste. Add reserved liquid and simmer for 3-4 minutes or until liquid reduces slightly. Stir in orange segments, coriander (cilantro) leaves and sugar. Serve scattered with spring onions.
Serves 4

Chinese barbecued or roasted duck is available from Oriental food stores which sell meat. If unavailable roast duck can be used instead.

CARDAMOM AND ORANGE DUCK

The curry pastes of Thailand are mixtures of freshly ground herbs and spices and if you are able to make your own it is well worth the small effort required.

THAI GREEN CHICKEN CURRY

1 tablespoon vegetable oil
2 onions, chopped
3 tablespoons Thai green curry paste
1 kg/2 lb boneless chicken thigh
or breast fillets, chopped

4 tablespoons fresh basil leaves
6 kaffir lime leaves, shredded
2¹/2 cups/600 mL/1 pt coconut milk
2 tablespoons Thai fish sauce (nam pla)
extra fresh basil leaves

1   Heat oil in a saucepan over a high heat, add onions and cook for 3 minutes or until golden. Stir in curry paste and cook for 2 minutes or until fragrant.

2   Add chicken, basil, lime leaves, coconut milk and fish sauce and bring to the boil. Reduce heat and simmer for 12-15 minutes or until chicken is tender and sauce is thick. Serve garnished with extra basil. **Serves 6**

▶ *Pea eggplant (aubergines) are tiny green eggplant (aubergines) about the size of green peas and are usually purchased still attached to the vine. They are used whole, eaten raw or cooked and have a bitter taste. If unavailable green peas can be used instead.*

MINTED BEAN CURRY

6 whole coriander (cilantro) plants, roots removedand washed, reserve leaves for another use
2 stalks fresh lemon grass, finely sliced, or
1 teaspoon dried lemon grass, soaked in hot water until soft
6 kaffir lime leaves, shredded
2 teaspoons palm or brown sugar
3 cups/750 mL/1¼ pt water
3 tablespoons Thai fish sauce (nam pla)
2 teaspoons peanut oil
3 small fresh green chillies, shredded (optional)

5 cm/2 in piece fresh ginger, shredded
2 teaspoons Thai green curry paste
220 g/7 oz pea eggplant (aubergines)
220 g/7 oz snake (yard-long) or green beans, cut into 2.5 cm/1 in pieces
440 g/14 oz canned tomatoes, drained and chopped
2 tablespoons tamarind concentrate
60 g/2 oz fresh mint leaves

1 Place coriander (cilantro) roots, lemon grass, lime leaves, sugar, water and fish sauce in a saucepan and bring to the boil. Reduce heat and simmer for 10 minutes. Strain, discard solids and set stock aside.

2 Heat oil in a wok or large saucepan over a medium heat, add chillies (if using), ginger and curry paste and stir-fry for 2-3 minutes or until fragrant. Add eggplant (aubergines) and beans and stir to coat with spice mixture. Stir in reserved stock and simmer for 10 minutes or until vegetables are tender. Add tomatoes and tamarind and simmer for 3 minutes or until hot. Stir in mint. **Serves 4**

GREEN CHILLI
and PRAWN CURRY

1 tablespoon vegetable oil
1.5 kg/3 lb medium uncooked prawns, shelled
and deveined, shells and heads reserved
2 stalks fresh lemon grass, bruised, or
1 teaspoon dried lemon grass, soaked
in hot water until soft
2 long fresh green chillies, halved
4 cm/1¹/₂ in piece fresh galangal or ginger,
or 6 slices bottled galangal
3 cups/750 mL/1¹/₄ pt water
2 teaspoons Thai green curry paste
1 cucumber, seeded and cut into thin strips
5 whole fresh green chillies (optional)
1 tablespoon palm or brown sugar
2 tablespoons Thai fish sauce (nam pla)
1 tablespoon coconut vinegar
2 teaspoons tamarind concentrate

1 Heat 2 teaspoons oil in a saucepan over a medium heat, add reserved prawn shells and heads and cook, stirring, for 3-4 minutes or until shells change colour. Add lemon grass, the halved green chillies, galangal or ginger and water and bring to the boil. Using a wooden spoon break up galangal or ginger, reduce heat and simmer for 10 minutes. Strain, discard solids and set stock aside.

2 Heat remaining oil in a wok or saucepan over a medium heat and stir-fry curry paste for 2-3 minutes or until fragrant.

3 Add prawns, cucumber, 5 whole green chillies (if using), sugar, reserved stock, fish sauce, vinegar and tamarind and cook, stirring, for 4-5 minutes or until prawns change colour and are cooked through. **Serves 4**

Fresh lemon grass is available from Oriental food shops and some supermarkets and greengrocers. It is also available dried; if using dried lemon grass soak it in hot water for 20 minutes or until soft before using. Lemon grass is also available in bottles from supermarkets, use this in the same way as you would fresh lemon grass.

> In Thailand curries are usually served over moulds of rice. The rice absorbs and is flavoured by the large proportion of liquid in the curry. The fragrant rices such as jasmine and basmati are perfect accompaniments for Thai curries.

RED BEEF CURRY

1 cup/250 ml/8 fl oz coconut cream
3 tablespoons Thai red curry paste
500 g/1 lb round or blade steak, cubed
155 g/5 oz pea eggplant (aubergines) or 1 eggplant (aubergine), diced
220 g/7 oz canned sliced bamboo shoots
6 kaffir lime leaves, crushed
1 tablespoon brown sugar
2 cups/500 ml/16 fl oz coconut milk
2 tablespoons Thai fish sauce (nam pla)
3 tablespoons fresh coriander (cilantro) leaves
2 fresh red chillies, chopped

1 Place coconut cream in a saucepan and bring to the boil over a high heat, then boil until oil separates from coconut cream and it reduces and thickens slightly. Stir in curry paste and boil for 2 minutes or until fragrant.

2 Add beef, eggplant (aubergines), bamboo shoots, lime leaves, sugar, coconut milk and fish sauce, cover and simmer for 35-40 minutes or until beef is tender. Stir in coriander (cilantro) and chillies. **Serves 4**

CASHEW *and* CHILLI BEEF CURRY

3 cm/1¼ in piece fresh galangal or ginger, chopped or 5 slices bottled galangal, chopped
1 stalk fresh lemon grass, finely sliced, or ½ teaspoon dried lemon grass, soaked in hot water until soft
3 kaffir lime leaves, finely shredded
2 small fresh red chillies, seeded and chopped
2 teaspoons shrimp paste
2 tablespoons Thai fish sauce (nam pla)
1 tablespoon lime juice
2 tablespoons peanut oil
4 red or golden shallots, sliced
2 cloves garlic, chopped
3 small fresh red chillies, sliced
500 g/1 lb round or blade steak, cut into 2 cm/3/4 in cubes
2 cups/500 ml/16 fl oz beef stock
250 g/8 oz okra, trimmed
60 g/2 oz cashews, roughly chopped
1 tablespoon palm or brown sugar
2 tablespoons light soy sauce

1 Place galangal or ginger, lemon grass, lime leaves, chopped chillies, shrimp paste, fish sauce and lime juice in a food processor and process to make a thick paste, adding a little water if necessary.

2 Heat 1 tablespoon oil in a wok or large saucepan over a medium heat, add shallots, garlic, sliced red chillies and spice paste and cook, stirring, for 2-3 minutes or until fragrant. Remove and set aside.

3 Heat remaining oil in wok over a high heat and stir-fry beef, in batches, until brown. Return spice paste to pan, stir in stock and okra and bring to the boil. Reduce heat and simmer, stirring occasionally, for 15 minutes.

4 Stir in cashews, sugar and soy sauce and simmer for 10 minutes longer or until beef is tender. **Serves 4**

RED BEEF

CURRY

Fish sauce 'nam pla' is characteristic of Thai cooking and appears as a seasoning in many dishes. Thai cooks take pride in making their own fish sauce and the ability to make a good sauce is the hallmark of an accomplished cook.

To store whole fresh coriander plants, place roots in 1 cm/1/2 in of water in a glass jar, cover coriander and jar with a plastic bag, secure bag around jar and store in the refrigerator. Coriander and other fresh herbs purchased in good condition will keep for a week or more when stored in this way. Do not wash the herbs before storing.

CHICKEN PHANAENG CURRY

2 cups/500 ml/16 fl oz coconut milk
3 tablespoons Thai red curry paste
500 g/1 lb chicken breast fillets, sliced
250 g/8 oz snake (yard-long) or
green beans
3 tablespoons unsalted peanuts, roasted
and finely chopped
2 teaspoons brown or palm sugar
1 tablespoon Thai fish sauce (nam pla)
1/2 cup/125 ml/4 fl oz coconut cream
2 tablespoons fresh basil leaves
2 tablespoons fresh coriander (cilantro) leaves
sliced fresh red chilli

1 Place coconut milk in a saucepan and bring to the boil over a high heat, then boil until oil separates from coconut milk and it reduces and thickens slightly. Stir in curry paste and boil for 2 minutes or until fragrant.

2 Add chicken, beans, peanuts, sugar and fish sauce and simmer for 5-7 minutes or until chicken is tender. Stir in coconut cream, basil and coriander(cilantro). Serve garnished with slices of chilli. **Serves 4**

CHICKEN WITH LIME *and* COCONUT

1 kg/2 lb chicken thigh or breast fillets, cut into thick strips
1 tablespoon Thai red curry paste
1 tablespoon vegetable oil
3 tablespoons palm or brown sugar
4 kaffir lime leaves
2 teaspoons finely grated lime rind
1 cup/250 ml/8 fl oz coconut cream
1 tablespoon Thai fish sauce (nam pla)
2 tablespoons coconut vinegar
3 tablespoons shredded coconut
4 fresh red chillies, sliced

1 Place chicken and curry paste in a bowl and toss to coat. Heat oil in a wok or large saucepan over a high heat, add chicken and stir-fry for 4-5 minutes or until lightly browned and fragrant.

2 Add sugar, lime leaves, lime rind, coconut cream and fish sauce and cook, stirring, over a medium heat for 3-4 minutes or until the sugar dissolves and caramelises.

3 Stir in vinegar and coconut and simmer until chicken is tender. Serve with chillies in a dish on the side. **Serves 4**

For something a little different serve this dish with egg noodles.

CHICKEN PHANAENG CURRY

▶ *Banana leaves are used in South-East Asian and Pacific countries in much the same way as Westerners use aluminium foil. Foil can be used if banana leaves are unavailable, however the finished dish will not have the flavour that the banana leaf contributes and it may be slightly drier.*

FISH WITH GREEN MANGO SAUCE

4 x 185 g/6 oz firm fish fillets or cutlets
4 pieces banana leaf, blanched
3 cloves garlic, sliced
1 tablespoon shredded fresh ginger
2 kaffir lime leaves, shredded
Green mango sauce
$1/2$ small green (unripe) mango, flesh grated
3 red or golden shallots, chopped
2 fresh red chillies, sliced
1 tablespoon brown sugar
$1/4$ cup/60 ml/2 fl oz water
1 tablespoon Thai fish sauce (nam pla)

1 Place a fish fillet or cutlet in the centre of each banana leaf. Top fish with a little each of the garlic, ginger and lime leaves, then fold over banana leaves to enclose. Place parcels over a charcoal barbecue or bake in the oven for 15-20 minutes or until fish flakes when tested with a fork.

2 To make sauce, place mango, shallots, chillies, sugar, water and fish sauce in a saucepan and cook, stirring, over a low heat for 4-5 minutes or until sauce is heated through.

3 To serve, place parcels on serving plates, cut open to expose fish and serve with sauce.

Serves 4

Oven temperature 180°C, 350°F, Gas 4 (optional)

DEEP-FRIED

DEEP-FRIED CHILLI FISH

2 x 500 g/1 lb whole fish such as bream, snapper, whiting, sea perch, cod or haddock, cleaned
4 fresh red chillies, chopped
4 fresh coriander (cilanto) roots
3 cloves garlic, crushed
1 teaspoon crushed black peppercorns
vegetable oil for deep-frying

CHILLI FISH

This dish is a stunning centrepiece for a Thai feast.

RED CHILLI SAUCE
²/₃ cup/170 g/5¹/₂ oz sugar
8 fresh red chillies, sliced
4 red or golden shallots, sliced
¹/₃ cup/90 ml/3 fl oz coconut vinegar
¹/₃ cup/90 ml/3 fl oz water

1 Make diagonal slashes along both sides of the fish.

2 Place chopped chillies, coriander (cilanto) roots, garlic and black peppercorns in a food processor and process to make a paste. Spread mixture over both sides of fish and marinate for 30 minutes.

3 To make sauce, place sugar, sliced chillies, shallots, vinegar and water in a saucepan and cook, stirring, over a low heat until sugar dissolves. Bring mixture to simmering and simmer, stirring occasionally, for 4 minutes or until sauce thickens.

4 Heat vegetable oil in a wok or deep-frying pan until a cube of bread dropped in browns in 50 seconds. Cook fish, one at a time, for 2 minutes each side or until crisp and flesh flakes when tested with a fork. Drain on absorbent kitchen paper. Serve with chilli sauce. **Serves 6**

SHELLFISH *with* LEMON GRASS

5 red or golden shallots, chopped
4 stalks fresh lemon grass, bruised and cut into
3 cm/1¹/₄ in pieces, or
2 teaspoons dried lemon grass, soaked in hot
water until soft
3 cloves garlic, chopped
5 cm/2 in piece fresh ginger, shredded
3 fresh red chillies, seeded and chopped
8 kaffir lime leaves, torn into pieces
750 g/1¹/₂ lb mussels, scrubbed
and beards removed
¹/₄ cup/60 mL/2 fl oz water
12 scallops on shells, cleaned
1 tablespoon lime juice

1 tablespoon Thai fish sauce (nam pla)
3 tablespoons fresh basil leaves

1 Place shallots, lemon grass, garlic, ginger, chillies and lime leaves in a small bowl and mix to combine.

2 Place mussels in a wok and sprinkle over half the shallot mixture. Pour in water, cover and cook over a high heat for 5 minutes.

3 Add scallops, remaining shallot mixture, lime juice, fish sauce and basil and toss to combine. Cover and cook for 4-5 minutes or until mussels and scallops are cooked. Discard any mussels that do not open after 5 minutes. **Serves 4**

Serve this dish at the table straight from the wok and don't forget to give each diner some of the delicious cooking juices.

► *Most Western kitchens contain the equipment required for Thai cooking. At its most basic a wok or large frying pan, several large saucepans, a food processor or a mortar and pestle and possibly a multi-layered steamer with a tight-fitting lid are all that is needed.*

FISH WITH LIME *and* GARLIC

750 g/1¹/₂ lb whole fish such as sea perch, sea bass, coral trout or snapper, cleaned
2 stalks fresh lemon grass, chopped, or 1 teaspoon dried lemon grass, soaked in hot water until soft
4 slices fresh ginger
1 fresh green chilli, halved
4 kaffir lime leaves, crushed
8 whole fresh coriander plants
Lime and garlic sauce
2 fresh red chillies, seeded and chopped
2 green chillies, seeded and chopped

3 cloves garlic, chopped
1 tablespoon shredded fresh ginger
1 cup/250 mL/8 fl oz fish or chicken stock
4 tablespoons lime juice
1 tablespoon Thai fish sauce (nam pla)

1 Cut deep diagonal slits in both sides of the fish. Place lemon grass, ginger, the halved green chilli, lime leaves and coriander plants in cavity of fish.

2 Half fill a wok with hot water and bring to the boil. Place fish on a wire rack and place above water. Cover wok and steam for 10-15 minutes or until flesh flakes when tested with a fork.

3 To make sauce, place red and green chillies, garlic, ginger, stock, lime juice and fish sauce in a small saucepan, bring to simmering over a low heat and simmer for 4 minutes. To serve, place fish on a serving plate and spoon over sauce. **Serves 4**

▶ *Many Thai recipes such as this one, and some of the others in this chapter and in the Snacks and Starters chapter, are great for barbecuing. For a memorable Thai-inspired barbecue meal, serve your favourite Thai barbecue dishes with a selection of Thai-style salads and dipping sauces. Other recipes suitable for barbecuing include Satay, Fish with Green Mango Sauce, Spiced Grilled Beef and Barbecued Pork Spare Ribs.*

CHARCOAL-GRILLED CHICKEN

1 kg/2 lb chicken pieces
4 fresh red chillies, chopped
4 cloves garlic, chopped
3 fresh coriander (cilanto) roots, chopped
2 stalks fresh lemon grass, chopped,
or 1 teaspoon dried lemon grass soaked
in hot water until soft
3 tablespoons lime juice
2 tablespoons light soy sauce
1 cup/250 ml/8 fl oz coconut cream
sweet chilli sauce

1 Place chicken in a ceramic or glass dish and set aside.

2 Place chillies, garlic, coriander (cilantro) roots, lemon grass, lime juice and soy sauce in a food processor and process to make paste. Mix paste with coconut cream and pour over chicken. Marinate for 1 hour.

3 Drain chicken and reserve marinade. Cook chicken over a slow charcoal or gas barbecue or under a preheated low grill, brushing frequently with reserved marinade, for 25-30 minutes or until chicken is tender. Serve with chilli sauce. **Serves 6**

CHICKEN *with* GARLIC AND PEPPER

4 cloves garlic
3 fresh coriander (cilanto) roots
1 teaspoon crushed black peppercorns
500 g/1 lb chicken breast fillets,
chopped into 3 cm/1¹/₄ in cubes
vegetable oil for deep-frying
30 g/1 oz fresh basil leaves
30 g/1 oz fresh mint leaves
sweet chilli sauce

1 Place garlic, coriander (cilantro) roots and black peppercorns in a food processor and process to make a paste. Coat chicken with garlic paste and marinate for 1 hour.

2 Heat oil in a wok or frying pan over a high heat until a cube of bread dropped in browns in 50 seconds, then deep-fry chicken, a few pieces at a time, for 2 minutes or until golden and tender. Drain on absorbent kitchen paper.

3 Deep-fry basil and mint until crisp, then drain and place on a serving plate. Top with chicken and serve with chilli sauce. **Serves 4**

Thai cooks use three types of basil in cooking – Asian sweet, holy and lemon – each has a distinctive flavour and is used for specific types of dishes. For this dish Asian sweet basil, known in Thailand as horapa, would be used.

WITH
AND PEPPER

> *In Thailand noodles are known as 'mee' and are frequently served as snacks.*

PAD THAI

315 g/10 oz fresh or dried rice noodles
2 teaspoons vegetable oil
4 red or golden shallots, chopped
3 fresh red chillies, chopped
2 tablespoons shredded fresh ginger
250 g/8 oz boneless chicken
breast fillets, chopped
250 g/8 oz medium uncooked prawns,
shelled and deveined
60 g/2 oz roasted peanuts, chopped
1 tablespoon sugar
4 tablespoons lime juice
3 tablespoons fish sauce
2 tablespoons light soy sauce
125 g/4 oz tofu, chopped

60 g/2 oz bean sprouts
4 tablespoons fresh coriander (cilantro) leaves
3 tablespoons fresh mint leaves
lime wedges to serve

1 Place noodles in a bowl and pour over boiling water to cover. If using fresh noodles soak for 2 minutes; if using dried noodles soak for 5-6 minutes or until soft. Drain well and set aside.

2 Heat oil in a frying pan or wok over a high heat, add shallots, chillies and ginger and stir-fry for 1 minute. Add chicken and prawns and stir-fry for 4 minutes or until cooked.

3 Add noodles, peanuts, sugar, lime juice and fish and soy sauces and stir-fry for 4 minutes or until heated through. Stir in tofu, bean sprouts, coriander (cilantro) and mint and cook for 1-2 minutes or until heated through. Serve with lime wedges. **Serves 4**

CHILLI FRIED RICE

2 teaspoons vegetable oil
2 fresh red chillies, chopped
1 tablespoon Thai red curry paste
2 onions, sliced
1¹/₂ cups/330 g/10¹/₂ oz rice, cooked
125 g/4 oz snake (yard-long)
or green beans, chopped
125 g/4 oz baby bok choy
(Chinese greens), blanched
3 tablespoons lime juice
2 teaspoons Thai fish sauce (nam pla)

1 Heat oil in a wok or frying pan over a high heat, add chillies and curry paste and stir-fry for 1 minute or until fragrant. Add onions and stir-fry for 3 minutes or until soft.

2 Add rice, beans and bok choy (Chinese greens) to pan and stir-fry for 4 minutes or until rice is heated through. Stir in lime juice and fish sauce.   **Serves 4**

This is a good way to turn leftover cooked rice into a tasty light meal.

CHILLI FRIED RICE

CELLOPHANE NOODLE SALAD

155 g/5 oz cellophane noodles
2 teaspoons sesame oil
2 cloves garlic, minced
1 tablespoon finely grated fresh ginger
500 g/1 lb pork mince
15 g/½ oz mint leaves
15 g/½ oz coriander (cilantro) leaves
8 lettuce leaves
5 red or golden shallots, chopped
1 fresh red chilli, sliced
2 tablespoons lemon juice
1 tablespoon light soy sauce

1 Place noodles in a bowl and pour over boiling water to cover. Stand for 10 minutes, then drain well.

2 Heat oil in a frying pan over a high heat, add garlic and ginger and stir-fry for 1 minute. Add pork and stir-fry for 5 minutes or until pork is browned and cooked through.

3 Arrange mint, coriander (cilantro), lettuce, shallots, chilli and noodles on a serving platter. Top with pork mixture, then drizzle with lemon juice and soy sauce.

Serves 4

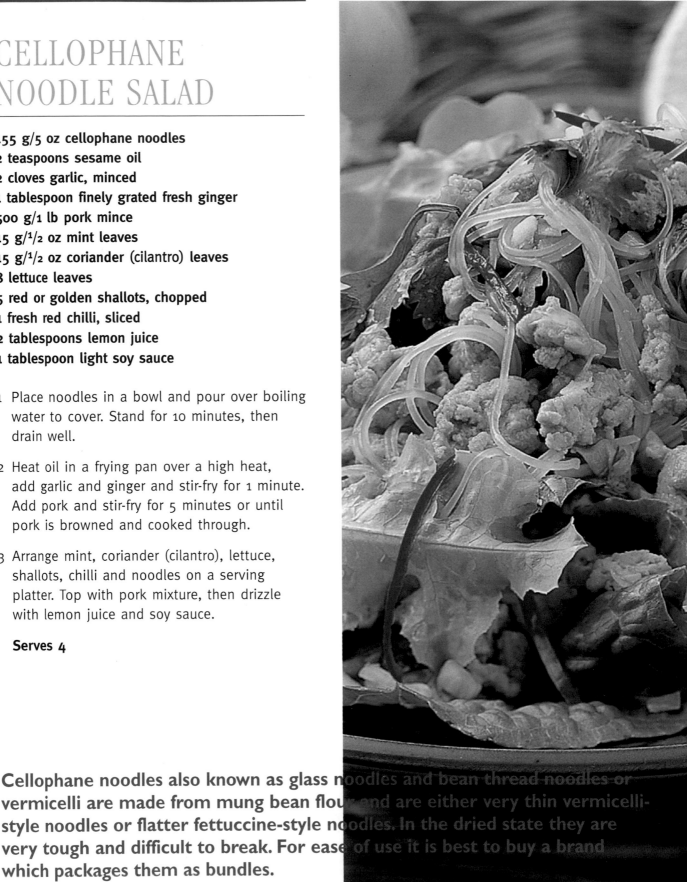

Cellophane noodles also known as glass noodles and bean thread noodles or vermicelli are made from mung bean flour and are either very thin vermicelli-style noodles or flatter fettuccine-style noodles. In the dried state they are very tough and difficult to break. For ease of use it is best to buy a brand which packages them as bundles.

▶ *Squash flowers or blossoms are very popular in Mexico where they are used in nearly every way imaginable. While it is the bright yellow pumpkin or winter squash flowers which are preferred by Mexican cooks, zucchini (courgette) flowers are an acceptable alternative. Serve this favourite soup with lime wedges.*

AZTEC FLOWER SOUP

2 teaspoons vegetable oil
1 onion, finely chopped
1 clove garlic, minced
2 tablespoons white rice
2 teaspoons chopped fresh marjoram
2 teaspoons chopped fresh thyme
8 cups/2 litres/3^1/$_2$ pt chicken stock
12 zucchini (courgette) flowers
440 g/14 oz cooked or canned chickpeas, rinsed and drained
250 g/8 oz chopped cooked chicken
1 avocado, sliced
2 jalapeño chillies, sliced
1 tablespoon fresh coriander (cilantro) leaves
^{1}/$_4$ onion, chopped

1 Heat oil in a saucepan over a medium heat, add onion and garlic and cook, stirring, for 3 minutes or until onion is soft. Add rice, marjoram, thyme and stock, bring to simmering and simmer for 15 minutes.

2 Remove the stamens and pistils from the zucchini (courgette) flowers by pinching with your fingers. Check that there are no insects hidden in the petals and wash flowers by dipping into water briefly. Trim stalks and set aside.

3 Add chickpeas, chicken and zucchini (courgette) flowers to soup and cook for 3 minutes or until flowers are tender.

4 To serve, ladle soup into bowls and top with avocado, chillies, coriander (cilantro) and onion. **Serves 6**

▶ *The ancho chilli is the favourite dried chilli of Mexican cooks. It is a mild to medium chilli and is the dried form of the poblano chilli. For an attractive presentation, decorate this dish with a swirl of sour cream and accompany with lime wedges.*

FETA-STUFFED ANCHO CHILLIES

6 ancho chillies
feta and goat's
cheese filling
500 g/1 lb soft feta cheese, crumbled
185 g/6 oz goat's cheese
4 tablespoons chopped fresh coriander (cilantro)
1 teaspoon ground cumin
1/3 cup/90 mL/3 fl oz lemon juice
Two-tomato salsa
250 g/8 oz cherry tomatoes, halved
250 g/8 oz yellow pear tomatoes, halved
1/2 red onion, sliced
1 tablespoon shredded fresh mint
crushed black peppercorns

1 Place chillies in a bowl, pour over hot water to cover and soak for 20 minutes or until soft. Drain chillies and discard water. Make a slit in each chilli and carefully remove seeds and membranes.

2 To make filling, place feta and goat's cheeses, coriander (cilantro), cumin and lemon juice in a bowl and mix to combine. Carefully spoon filling into chillies and place in a baking dish. Pour a little water into baking dish, cover and bake for 20 minutes or until heated through.

3 To make salsa, place tomatoes, onion, mint and black pepper to taste in bowl and toss to combine. To serve, divide salsa between serving plates and top with a chilli. **Serves 6**

Oven temperature 200°C, 400°F, Gas 6

BEEF TOSTADA CUPS

vegetable oil for deep-frying
8 corn tortillas
Beef Filling
2 teaspoons mild chilli powder
1 teaspoon ground cumin
1/4 cup/60 ml/2 fl oz lime juice
500 g/1 lb rump steak, trimmed of visible fat
2 red onions, sliced
1/2 bunch coriander

1 Heat oil in a saucepan until a cube of bread dropped in browns in 50 seconds. Deep-fry tortillas, one at a time pressed between two metal ladles, for 1 minute or until crisp and golden. Drain on absorbent kitchen paper.

2 To make filling, place chilli powder, cumin and lime juice in a glass or ceramic dish and mix to combine. Add steak, turn to coat and marinate for 5 minutes. Drain steak and cook on a preheated barbecue or under a grill for 2-3 minutes each side or until cooked to your liking. Rest steak for 2 minutes, then cut into strips and place in a bowl. Add onions and coriander (cilantro) leaves and toss to combine.

3 To serve, divide filling between tostada cups and serve immediately. **Makes 8**

Serve these tasty snacks with salsas of your choice and lime wedges.

NEW MEXICO ENCHILADAS

6 corn or flour tortillas
1/3 cup/90 mL/3 fl oz chilli sauce
45 g/1½ oz grated tasty cheese (mature Cheddar)

Cheese and Spinach Filling
2 teaspoons vegetable oil
1 onion, chopped
2 fresh green or red chillies, chopped
1 teaspoon cumin seeds
½ bunch/250 g/8 oz silverbeet or English spinach, leaves shredded
3 tomatoes, peeled and chopped
2 potatoes, cooked and chopped
155 g/5 oz feta cheese, crumbled
125 g/4 oz grated tasty cheese (mature Cheddar)

1 To make filling, heat oil in a nonstick frying pan over a medium heat, add onion, chillies and cumin seeds and cook, stirring, for 4 minutes or until onion is golden and soft. Add silverbeet or spinach, tomatoes and potatoes and cook for 4 minutes or until silverbeet or spinach wilts and mixture is heated through. Stir in feta cheese and 125 g/ 4 oz of the tasty cheese (mature Cheddar).

2 Warm tortillas in a dry frying pan over a medium heat for 20-30 seconds or until heated through. Remove from pan, spread with a little chilli sauce and place in a baking dish. Top with some of the filling then another tortilla. Repeat layers to use all the filling and tortillas. Scatter tortilla stack with remaining tasty cheese (mature Cheddar) and bake for 20 minutes or until cheese melts and filling is heated. To serve, cut into wedges. **Serves 4** *Oven temperature 180°C, 350°F, Gas 4*

Corn tortillas are the traditional bread of the Aztec, Maya and other Mexican-Indians. The most readily available tortillas outside of Central and South America are made from yellow or blue cornmeal or wheat flour.

NEW MEXICO ENCHILADAS

▶ *This variation of a Mexican favourite, chillies rellenos, bakes rather than fries the stuffed chillies, making it a healthier and easier option for the home cook. If poblano chillies are unavailable choose another mild chilli such as New Mexico or one of the wax or banana chillies.*

STUFFED POBLANO CHILLIES

12 poblano chillies

Beef and Bean Filling
2 teaspoons vegetable oil
1 onion, chopped
315 g/10 oz beef mince
185 g/6 oz cooked or canned pinto beans, rinsed and drained
pinch cayenne pepper
¹/₂ cup/125 ml/4 fl oz tomato purée

TOMATILLO SAUCE
2 x 315 g/10 oz canned tomatillos, drained and finely chopped
1 onion, chopped
3 tablespoons chopped fresh coriander
¹/₂ cup/125 ml/4 fl oz vegetable stock

1 Place chillies in a hot frying pan or comal and cook until skins are blistered and charred. Place in a plastic food bag and stand for 10 minutes or until cool enough to handle. Carefully remove skins from chillies and cut a slit in the side of each one. Carefully remove seeds and membranes and set aside.

2 To make filling, heat oil in a frying pan over a medium heat, add onion and cook, stirring, for 2 minutes or until soft. Add beef and cook, stirring, for 3-4 minutes or until brown. Stir in beans, cayenne pepper and tomato purée, bring to simmering and simmer for 5 minutes or until mixture reduces and thickens. Spoon filling into chillies and place in a baking dish.

3 To make sauce, place tomatillos, onion, coriander (cilantro) and stock in a saucepan, bring to simmering and simmer for 5 minutes or until sauce reduces and thickens. Pour sauce over chillies and bake for 25 minutes or until chillies are heated through. **Makes 12**

Oven temperature 180°C, 350°F, Gas 4

1 Place chillies a hot frying pan or comal and cook until skins are blistered and charred.

2 Spoon filling into chillies and place in a baking dish.

3 Pour sauce over chillies and bake for 25 minutes or until heated through.

STUFFED
POBLANO CHILLIES

*Warming tortillas before folding or rolling makes them pliable and prevents breaking or cracking.
To warm tortillas, place in a dry frying pan over a medium heat for 20-30 seconds each side.
Alternatively, wrap the tortillas in aluminium foil and heat in a low oven or place in a covered
container and heat in the microwave. Serve taquitos with Salsa Verde.*

PORK *and* MARJORAM TAQUITOS

12 corn tortillas, warmed
vegetable oil for shallow-frying
Pork and Marjoram Filling
1 teaspoon vegetable oil
1 onion, chopped
2 fresh red chillies, chopped
2 cloves garlic, crushed
2 teaspoons ground cumin
500 g/1 lb pork mince
3 tablespoons chopped fresh marjoram

1 To make filling, heat oil in a frying pan over a high heat, add onion, chillies, garlic and cumin and cook, stirring, for 3 minutes or until onion and chillies are soft. Add pork and cook, stirring, for 3-4 minutes or until brown. Remove pan from heat, stir in marjoram and cool slightly.

2 Place 1 tablespoon of filling along the centre of each tortilla, then roll up and secure with wooden toothpicks or cocktail sticks.

3 Heat 1 cm/$1/2$ in oil in a frying pan until a cube of bread dropped in browns in 50 seconds. Cook taquitos, a few at a time, for 1-2 minutes or until crisp. Drain on absorbent kitchen paper. **Makes 12**

CHICKEN *and* CHILLI TAMALES

30 dried corn husks
Tamale Dough
125 g/4 oz butter, softened
750 g/1¹/₂ lb fresh masa
2 tablespoons baking powder
3/4 cup/185 mL/6 fl oz chicken stock
Chicken and Green Chilli Filling
1 tablespoon vegetable oil
2 fresh green chillies, chopped
1 tablespoon fresh oregano leaves
1 clove garlic, crushed
250 g/8 oz finely chopped chicken
1 tablespoon flour
1 tablespoon tomato paste (purée)

1 Place corn husks in a bowl, pour over warm water to cover and soak for 30 minutes.

2 To make dough, place butter in a bowl and beat until light and creamy. Place masa and baking powder in a bowl, then stir in stock and mix to combine. Gradually beat masa mixture into butter and continue beating to make a smooth dough.

3 To make filling, heat a frying pan over a high heat, add oil, chillies, oregano and garlic and cook, stirring, for 1 minute. Stir in chicken, flour and tomato paste (purée) and cook, stirring, for 5 minutes or until chicken is cooked and mixture reduces and thickens.

4 Drain corn husks and pat dry with absorbent kitchen paper. Take 2 tablespoons of Tamale Dough and press to flatten, place on a corn husk, then top with 1 tablespoon of filling. Take another 2 tablespoons of dough press to flatten, then place over filling and press edges of dough to enclose. Fold corn husk around dough parcel to enclose, then wrap other husk around the parcel in the opposite

direction and tie to secure. Repeat with remaining corn husks, dough and filling to make 15 tamales.

5 Place tamales in a steamer over boiling water and steam for 45 minutes or until cooked through. **Makes 15**

Serve these tasty morsels with Salsa Ranchera. Fresh masa can be purchased from Mexican specialty food shops or wholesalers.

CHICKEN TORTILLAS

2 cloves garlic, minced
1 teaspoon ground cumin
1/2 teaspoon chilli powder
1/3 cup/90 ml/3 fl oz lime juice
1 tablespoon tequila
4 boneless chicken breast fillets
12 corn tortillas
1 red onion, sliced
1/2 bunch fresh coriander (cilantro)
Guacamole
Roasted Chilli Salsa
1/2 cup/125 g/4 oz sour cream (optional)

1 Place garlic, cumin, chilli powder, lime juice and tequila in a bowl and mix to combine. Add chicken, turn to coat, then cover and marinate for 30 minutes.

2 Drain chicken and cook on a preheated hot barbecue or char-grill or in a frying pan for 3-4 minutes each side or until golden and cooked through. Cut chicken into slices.

3 Warm tortillas in a dry frying pan over a medium heat for 20-30 seconds each side or until heated through.

4 To serve, top each tortilla with chicken, onion and coriander (cilantro) leaves, fold or roll and accompany with bowls of Guacamole, salsa and sour cream, if using. **Makes 12**

CHEESE *and* BEAN QUESADILLAS

155 g/5 oz cooked or canned black
or black-eyed beans, drained
60 g/2 oz grated mozzarella cheese
60 g/2 oz grated tasty cheese
(mature Cheddar)
2 tablespoons hot chilli sauce
12 flour tortillas, warmed
1 egg white
vegetable oil

1 Place beans, mozzarella cheese, tasty cheese (mature Cheddar) and chilli sauce in a bowl and mix to combine.

2 Place 2 tablespoons of mixture on one-half of each tortilla. Brush edges with egg white and fold to enclose filling. Press edges together firmly to seal.

3 Brush quesadillas with a little oil and cook in a preheated dry frying pan over a medium heat for 2 minutes each side or until puffed and golden. **Makes 12**

Serve with Roasted Chilli Salsa or Salsa Mexicana
Serve empanadas with Salsa Mexicana or Salsa
Ranchera and lime wedges.
If lemon thyme is unavailable use ordinary thyme
and a little finely grated lemon rind.

CHEESE AND
BEAN

Beef, pork and lamb steaks are also delicious prepared in this way. Adjust the cooking times to suit the meat you are using and according to personal taste.

QUESADILLAS

PRAWN EMPANADAS

Vegetable oil for deep-frying
Empanada Dough
2³/₄ cups/350 g/11 oz flour
60 g/2 oz soft butter
³/₄ cup/185 ml/6 fl oz warm water
Chilli and Prawn Filling
2 teaspoons vegetable oil
1 onion, chopped
1 tablespoon fresh oregano leaves
2 teaspoons fresh lemon thyme leaves
500 g/1 lb peeled uncooked prawns
2 green tomatoes, peeled and chopped
4 poblano chillies, roasted, seeded and peeled
and chopped

1 To make dough, place flour and butter in
   a food processor and process until mixture
   resembles coarse breadcrumbs. With machine
   running, add enough of the warm water to
   form a smooth dough. Knead dough on a
   lightly floured surface for 3 minutes, then
   divide into 12 portions. Cover with a damp
   cloth and set aside.

2 To make filling, heat oil in a frying pan over
   medium heat, add onion, oregano and thyme
   and cook for 4 minutes or until onions are
   golden. Add prawns, tomatoes and chillies
   and simmer for 5 minutes or until mixture
   reduces and thickens. Cool.

3 Roll each portion of dough out to form an
   18 cm/7 in circle about 3 mm/¹/₈ in thick.
   Place 3 tablespoons of filling on one half of
   each dough round, then fold over to enclose
   filling and pinch edges to seal.

4 Heat oil in a saucepan until a cube of bread
   dropped in browns in 50 seconds, then cook
   empanadas, a few at a time, for 2-3 minutes
   or until crisp and golden. Drain on absorbent
   kitchen paper and serve. **Makes 12**

PINTO BEAN SOUP

185 g/6 oz dried pinto beans, soaked overnight
and drained
1 onion, quartered
3 tomatoes, roasted and peeled
1 poblano chilli, roasted and peeled
4 cloves garlic
6 cups/1.5 litres/2^1/$_2$ pt water
2-3 cups/500-750 ml/16 fl oz-1^1/$_4$ pt chicken
or vegetable stock
vegetable oil for shallow-frying
6 day-old flour or corn tortillas,
cut into strips
2 ancho chillies, seeded
155 g/5 oz feta cheese, crumbled
2 tablespoons fresh coriander (cilantro) leaves

1 Place beans, onion, tomatoes, poblano chilli,
   garlic and water in a saucepan. Bring to the
   boil and boil for 10 minutes, then reduce
   heat and simmer for 1 hour or until beans are
   tender. Cool slightly, then purée beans and
   vegetables with cooking liquid in a food
   processor or blender.

2 Return purée to a clean saucepan, stir in
   stock, bring to simmering and simmer,
   stirring, for 10-15 minutes.

3 Heat 1 cm/^{1}/$_2$ in oil in a frying pan until a
   cube of bread dropped in browns in 50
   seconds and cook tortilla strips until golden
   and crisp. Drain on absorbent kitchen paper.
   Add ancho chillies to pan and cook until
   crisp, then drain and cut into thin strips.

4 To serve, ladle soup into warm bowls. Arrange
   tortilla and chilli strips, feta cheese and
   coriander (cilantro) on a serving platter and
   pass with soup to garnish. **Serves 6**

PINTO BEAN SOUP

▶ *Salsas, chillies, lime juice and lime wedges are standard accompaniments to any Mexican meal.*

PRAWN TOSTADITAS

Vegetable oil
8 corn tortillas
1/2 avocado, chopped
2 tablespoons shredded fresh mint
Prawn and Vegetable Topping
1 cob sweet corn
1 red capsicum (pepper), quartered
1 yellow capsicum (pepper), quartered
1 red onion, cut into wedges
375 g/12 oz medium uncooked prawns, shelled and deveined
4 mild fresh green chillies, cut into strips
1 tablespoon lime juice

1 To make topping, place sweet corn cob and red and yellow capsicums(peppers) on a preheated hot barbecue or char-grill and cook until lightly charred. Cut corn from cob and set aside.Cut capsicums (peppers) into strips and set aside.

2 Heat 2 teaspoons of oil in a frying pan over a medium heat, add onion and cook for 4 minutes or until golden. Add prawns, chillies and lime juice and cook for 2 minutes or until prawns change colour. Add sweet corn kernels and red and yellow capsicums (peppers), toss to combine and set aside.

3 Heat 2.5 cm/1 in oil in a frying pan over a medium heat until a cube of bread dropped in browns in 50 seconds. Cook tortillas, one at time, for 45 seconds each side or until crisp. Drain on absorbent kitchen paper.

4 To serve, pile topping onto tortillas, then scatter with avocado and mint. Serve immediately. **Serves 4**

BARBECUE CHILLI PRAWNS

1 kg/2 lb medium uncooked prawns, in their shells
250 g/8 oz chopped pawpaw
2 tablespoons chopped fresh mint
lime wedges
sliced chillies
Orange Marinade
2 tablespoons mild chilli powder

2 tablespoons chopped fresh oregano
2 cloves garlic, crushed
2 teaspoons grated orange rind
2 teaspoons grated lime rind
1/4 cup/60 mL/2 fl oz orange juice
1/4 cup/60 mL/2 fl oz lime juice

1 To make marinade, place chilli powder, oregano, garlic, orange and lime rinds and orange and lime juices in a bowl and mix to combine. Add prawns, toss, cover and marinate in the refrigerator for 1 hour.

2 Drain prawns and cook on a preheated hot char-grill or barbecue plate (griddle) for 1 minute each side or until they change colour.

3 Place pawpaw and mint in bowl and toss to combine. To serve, pile prawns onto serving plates, top with pawpaw mixture and accompany with lime wedges and sliced chillies. **Serves 4**

Cooking the prawns in their shells results in them being more tender and juicy. However, if you prefer the prawns can be peeled before marinating.

CUE CHILLI PRAWNS

1 Place corn husks in a bowl, pour over warm water to cover and soak for 30 minutes.

2 Cut fish fillets in half and spread both sides with chilli paste.

3 Place fish on top of corn husks, then cover with more husks, fold to enclose fish and tie to secure.

▶ *Corn husks and banana leaves are used extensively in Mexico as wrappers for edible parcels. Corn husks are favoured in northern Mexico while banana leaves are more popular in southern and coastal areas.*

FISH BAKED *in* CORN HUSKS

16-24 dried corn husks
4 firm white fish fillets
3 tablespoons fresh coriander (cilantro) leaves
1 avocado, sliced
pickled jalapeño chillies
corn or flour tortillas, warmed
Chilli lime paste
3 cloves garlic, chopped
2 mild fresh green chillies, chopped
2 tablespoons fresh oregano leaves
2 tablespoons mild chilli powder
2 teaspoons grated lime rind
1 teaspoon ground cumin
1/4 cup/60 ml/2 fl oz lime juice

1 Place corn husks in a bowl, pour over warm water to cover and soak for 30 minutes.

2 To make chilli paste, place garlic, chillies, oregano, chilli powder, lime rind, cumin and lime juice in a food processor or blender and process until smooth.

3 Cut each fish fillet in half, then spread both sides with chilli paste.

4 Overlap 2-3 corn husks, place a piece of fish on top, then cover with more husks, fold to enclose fish and tie to secure. Place parcels on a baking tray and bake for 10-12 minutes or until flesh flakes when tested with a fork.

5 To serve, open fish parcels, scatter with coriander (cilantro) and accompany with avocado, chillies and tortillas. **Serves 4**

Oven temperature 180°C, 350°F, Gas 4

FISH BAKED
IN CORN HUSKS

ROASTED GARLIC FISH

1.5 kg/3 lb whole fish such as bream, snapper, whiting, sea perch, cod or haddock, cleaned
1 lemon, sliced
2 fresh red chillies, halved
3 sprigs fresh marjoram
7 cloves garlic, unpeeled
30 g/1 oz butter
¹/₃ cup/90 mL/3 fl oz coconut milk

1 Pat fish dry with absorbent kitchen paper. Place fish in a baking dish and fill cavity with lemon slices, chillies and marjoram sprigs.

2 Place garlic in a hot frying pan or comal and cook until skins are charred and garlic is soft. Squeeze garlic from skins into a bowl, add butter and mix to combine. Spread garlic butter over both sides of fish, cover with foil and bake for 40 minutes or until flesh flakes when tested with a fork. Remove foil, place under a hot grill and cook for 3-4 minutes each side or until skin is crisp.
To serve, drizzle with coconut milk. **Serves 4**

Oven temperature 150°C, 300°F, Gas 2

Serve fish with Mexican Red Rice or tortillas and a salad.

ROASTED GARLIC FISH

GRILLED SCALLOPS *with* SALSA

30 scallops
chilli or lime oil
crisp tortilla chips
Pineapple salsa
125 g/4 oz chopped pineapple
¹/₄ red capsicum (pepper), finely chopped
2 medium green chillies, chopped
1 tablespoon fresh coriander (cilantro) leaves
1 tablespoon fresh mint leaves
1 tablespoon lime juice

1 To make salsa, place pineapple, red pepper, chillies, coriander (cilantro), mint and lime juice ina bowl, toss to combine, then stand for 20 minutes.

2 Brush scallops with oil and cook on a preheated hot char-grill or barbecue plate (griddle) for 30 seconds each side or until they just change colour. Serve immediately with salsa and tortilla chips. **Serves 4**

To make crisp tortilla chips, cut day-old tortillas into wedges and shallow fry for 1-2 minutes or until crisp.

SEAFOOD TACOS

8 flour tortillas, warmed
155 g/5 oz feta cheese crumbled
Seafood Filling
2 teaspoons vegetable oil
1 onion, chopped
2 tomatoes, chopped
375 g/12 oz white fish, cubed
250 g/8 oz shelled and deveined medium uncooked prawns
12 scallops
3 medium fresh green chillies, chopped
2 tablespoons chopped fresh oregano
1 teaspoon finely grated lemon rind

1 To make filling, heat oil in a frying pan over a high heat, add onion and cook for 4 minutes or until golden. Add tomatoes and cook for 5 minutes. Add fish, prawns, scallops, chillies, oregano and lemon rind and cook, tossing, for 3-4 minutes or until seafood is cooked.

2 To serve, spoon filling down the centre of each tortilla and scatter with feta cheese. Fold tortilla to enclose filling and serve immediately. **Serves 4**

These indulgent tacos are wonderful served with Garlic and Chilli Salsa.

▶ *Known in Mexico as Veracruzana sauce and originating from the region of Veracruz, the sauce in this recipe is traditionally served with and used as a cooking sauce for fish fillets and whole fish. It is also delicious served with grilled lamb or veal chops.*

SKEWERS *with* TOMATO SAUCE

750 g/1½ lb white fish, cubed
¼ cup/60 ml/2 fl oz lime juice
freshly ground black pepper
6 corn or flour tortillas, warmed
2 tablespoons chopped fresh coriander (cilantro)
lime wedges
Tomato, olive and
caper sauce
1 tablespoon olive oil
1 onion, finely chopped
1 clove garlic, minced
4 ripe tomatoes, chopped

90 g/3 oz green olives
2 jalapeño chillies, chopped
2 tablespoons capers, drained
2 tablespoons chopped fresh flat
leaf parsley

1 Thread fish onto six lightly oiled skewers, brush with lime juice and season with black pepper to taste. Set aside.

2 To make sauce, heat oil in a frying pan over a medium heat, add onion and garlic and cook, stirring, for 2 minutes or until onion is soft. Add tomatoes, olives, chillies, capers and parsley and cook, stirring, for 5 minutes or until sauce is warm. Season with black pepper to taste.

3 Cook fish skewers on a preheated hot barbecue or char-grill for 1 minute each side or until tender. To serve, place fish skewers on tortillas, spoon over sauce, scatter with coriander (cilantro) and accompany with lime wedges.

Serves 6

SPICED MUSSELS IN VINEGAR

SPICED MUSSELS *in* VINEGAR

2 teaspoons vegetable oil
2 onions, chopped
3 medium fresh green chillies, chopped
1 tablespoon chopped fresh oregano
1 teaspoon ground cumin
1/2 teaspoon crushed black peppercorns
3 bay leaves
1 cinnamon stick
1/4 cup/60 mL/2 fl oz apple cider vinegar
1 1/2 cups/375 mL/12 fl oz fish stock
1 kg/2 lb mussels in shells, scrubbed
and beards removed

1 Heat oil in a saucepan over a medium heat, add onions and cook, stirring, for 3 minutes or until soft. Add chillies, oregano, cumin, peppercorns, bay leaves and cinnamon and cook, stirring, for 2 minutes.

2 Stir vinegar and stock into pan and bring to the boil. Add mussels, bring to simmering, cover and simmer for 5 minutes or until mussels open. Discard any mussels that do not open after 5 minutes cooking. Serve mussels with pan juices. **Serves 4**

Try this recipe using clams, cleaned baby octopus or squid.

FISH *with* MARINATED ONIONS

4 firm white fish fillets
1/2 cup/60 g/2 oz flour
1 tablespoon ground cumin
1 tablespoon mild chilli powder
2 teaspoons ground coriander
2 tablespoons vegetable oil
Lime marinated onions
3 white onions, thinly sliced
3 tablespoons fresh coriander (cilantro) leaves
1 tablespoon sugar
1/2 cup/125 ml/4 fl oz lime juice

1 To make marinated onions, place onions, coriander (cilanto) leaves, sugar and lime juice in a bowl, cover and marinate at room temperature for at least 1 hour.

2 Place fish fillets on absorbent kitchen paper and pat dry. Place flour, cumin, chilli powder and ground coriander in a plastic food bag and toss to combine. Add fish and toss to coat with spice mixture, then shake off excess.

3 Heat oil in a frying pan over a medium heat, add fish and cook for 1-2 minutes each side or until flesh flakes when tested with a fork. Serve with marinated onions. **Serves 4**

This simple fish dish is delicious served with roasted tomatoes and red and green peppers.

MARINATED LIME FISH

625 g/1 1/4 lb firm white fish fillets, cut into strips
1 cup/250 ml/8 fl oz lime juice
3 ripe tomatoes, chopped
4 pickled jalapeño chillies, sliced
1 tablespoon chopped fresh oregano
1/3 cup/90 ml/3 fl oz olive oil
1/2 onion, finely diced
3 tablespoons chopped stuffed olives
2 tablespoons fresh coriander (cilanto) leaves

1 Place fish in a bowl, pour over lime juice and marinate in the refrigerator, tossing occasionally, for 3 hours or until fish is opaque. Drain off half the lime juice, then add tomatoes, chillies, oregano and oil. Toss and chill for 1 hour longer.

2 Before serving, stand at room temperature for 20 minutes, then scatter with onion, olives and coriander (cilanto).

Serves 6

MARINATED LIME

FISH

Known the world over as ceviche or seviche this classic Mexican fish dish must be made
with the freshest fish (never ever frozen). Any firm fleshed fish can be used and prawns,
scallops, crab or lobster are delicious and elegant alternatives.

SPICED SHREDDED BEEF

750 g/1¹/₂ lb boneless beef chuck, blade or brisket, trimmed of visible fat
1 onion, halved
2 cloves garlic, peeled
1 clove
2 teaspoons cumin seeds
8 cups/2 litres/3¹/₂ pt water
Green Chilli and Tomato Sauce
2 teaspoons vegetable oil
1 onion, chopped
2 hot green chillies, chopped
440 g/14 oz canned tomatoes, undrained and chopped

1 Place beef, onion, garlic, clove, cumin seeds and water in a saucepan over a medium heat, bring to simmering and simmer, skimming the top occasionally, for 1¹/₂ hours or until beef is very tender. Remove pan from heat and cool beef in liquid. Skim fat from surface as it cools. Remove beef from liquid and shred with a fork. Reserve cooking liquid for making sauce.

2 To make sauce, heat oil in a frying pan over a high heat, add onion and chillies and cook, stirring, for 3 minutes or until tender. Stir in tomatoes and 1 cup/250 mL/8 fl oz of the reserved cooking liquid, bring to simmering and simmer for 10 minutes or until mixture reduces and thickens.

3 Add shredded beef to sauce and simmer for 5 minutes or until heated through. **Serves 6**

The cooking time will depend on the cut of meat used. For a complete meal, serve on warm flour tortillas with salad and Green Rice with Herbs.

> *Banana leaves are a popular wrapper in southern and coastal Mexico. Corn husks or aluminium foil can be used instead, but the dish will lack the flavour imparted by the banana leaves.*

CHICKEN IN BANANA LEAVES

**2 whole chicken breasts on the bone,
skin removed**
4 large banana leaves
4 spring onions, chopped
3 tablespoons fresh coriander (cilanto) leaves
Spice mixture
3 New Mexico chillies
1 cup/250 ml/8 fl oz water
2 hot fresh green chillies, chopped
3 cloves garlic, chopped
2 tablespoons sweet paprika
1 tablespoon fresh oregano leaves
2 teaspoons ground cumin
2 teaspoons finely grated orange rind
2 tablespoons lemon juice

1 To make spice mixture, place chillies in a hot frying pan or comal and cook until skins are blistered and charred. Transfer chillies to a bowl, pour over water and soak for 30 minutes.

2 Drain chillies and discard soaking liquid. Place soaked chillies, green chillies, garlic, paprika, oregano, cumin, orange rind and lemon juice in a food processor or blender and process to make a paste.

3 Cut chicken breasts in half and spread each with spice mixture. Warm banana leaves by holding over a gas flame or heating in the microwave until pliable. Place a piece of chicken on each banana leaf, top with any remaining spice mixture and scatter over spring onions and coriander(cilanto). Fold banana leaves around chicken to enclose and tie to secure. Place parcels in a glass or ceramic dish and marinate in the refrigerator for 3 hours or overnight.

4 Transfer chicken parcels to a baking dish and bake for 25-35 minutes or until chicken is tender. **Serves 4**

Oven temperature 160°C, 325°F, Gas 3

CHICKEN *in* PUMPKIN SEED SAUCE

4 boneless chicken breast fillets
¹/₂ onion
2 cloves garlic
2 stalks fresh coriander (cilanto)
4 cups/1 litre/13/4 pt water
Pumpkin seed Sauce
2 x 440 g/14 oz canned tomatillos, drained
12 serrano chillies
¹/₂ bunch fresh coriander (cilanto)
¹/₄ onion, chopped
1 clove garlic
1¹/₂ cups/45 g/1¹/₂ oz green
pumpkin seeds (pepitas)
3 tablespoons unsalted peanuts

1 Place chicken, onion, garlic, coriander (cilanto) stalks and water in a saucepan over a low heat, bring to simmering and simmer for 15 minutes. Remove chicken from liquid. Strain cooking liquid and discard solids. Reserve liquid for sauce.

2 To make sauce, place tomatillos, chillies, coriander (cilanto) leaves, onion and garlic in a food processor or blender and process until smooth.

3 Heat a frying pan over a medium heat, add pumpkin seeds (pepitas) and cook, stirring, for 3-4 minutes or until seeds pop and are golden. Place pumpkin seeds (pepitas) and peanuts in a clean food processor or blender and process to make a paste. Return nut paste to frying pan and cook, stirring, for 3 minutes or until golden. Gradually stir in tomatillo mixture and 2 cups/500 mL/16 fl oz of the reserved cooking liquid, bring to simmering and simmer, stirring frequently, for 10 minutes. Add chicken to sauce and simmer for 5 minutes or until heated through. **Serves 4**

If the sauce is too thick add cooking liquid to achieve the desired consistency.
Canned serrano chillies can be used in place of fresh if you wish.

ROASTED CHILLI DUCK

2.5 kg/5 lb duck
sea salt
crushed black peppercorns
1 orange, halved
1 head garlic, cloves separated
2 tablespoons mild chilli powder
2 tablespoons sweet paprika
3 cloves garlic, crushed
2 tablespoons tequila
3 tablespoons chopped fresh mint

1 Pierce skin of duck all over with a fork, then rub with salt and black pepper and place on a rack set in a baking dish. Place orange and garlic cloves in cavity of bird and bake for 30 minutes. Drain juices from pan.

2 Combine chilli powder, paprika, crushed garlic and tequila and rub over duck. Reduce oven temperature to 180°C/350°F/Gas 4 and bake for 40 minutes or until skin is crisp and meat is tender. Just prior to serving, scatter with mint.

Serves 4

Oven temperature 220°C, 425°F, Gas 7

Serve with a pile of warm flour tortillas and a selection of salsas.

ROASTED
CHILLI DUCK

CRISPY LAMB TORTILLA PIZZA

500 g/1 lb fresh masa
315 g/10 oz Refried Beans
315 g/10 oz feta cheese, crumbled
1 cup/250 mL/8 fl oz Enchilada Sauce
lime wedges
chopped fresh chillies
Twice-Cooked Lamb
1.5 kg/3 lb leg lamb
1 onion, halved
2 cloves garlic
3 sprigs fresh oregano
$^1/_2$ teaspoon cumin seeds
chilli powder

1 To cook lamb, place lamb, onion, garlic, oregano and cumin seeds in a saucepan and pour over enough water to cover. Bring to the boil, cover, reduce heat and simmer for $1^1/_2$ hours or until very tender. Drain lamb and place in a baking dish. Sprinkle with chilli powder and bake for 30 minutes. Shred lamb and set aside.

2 Take 4 tablespoons masa, place between sheets of nonstick baking paper and roll out to form a large, very thin round. Place tortilla in a hot dry frying pan or comal and cook for 3 minutes each side or until crisp. Keep warm while cooking remaining tortillas.

3 Spread tortillas with beans, then top with shredded lamb, feta cheese and Enchilada Sauce and bake for 10 minutes or until topping is heated through. Serve with lime wedges and chopped chillies. **Serves 4**

Oven temperature 180°C, 350°F, Gas 4

SLOW-BAKED CHILLI LAMB

1.5 kg/3 lb leg lamb, trimmed of visible fat
Chilli herb paste
4 ancho chillies
3 cloves garlic, unpeeled
1 ripe tomato, peeled and chopped
1 tablespoon chopped fresh oregano
$^1/_2$ teaspoon ground cumin
$^1/_2$ teaspoon crushed black peppercorns
2 tablespoons apple cider vinegar

1 To make chilli paste, place chillies and garlic in a hot dry frying pan or comal over a high heat and cook until skins are blistered and charred. Place chillies in a bowl, pour over hot water to cover and soak for 30 minutes. Drain chillies and discard water.

2 Squeeze garlic from skins. Place chillies, garlic, tomato, oregano, cumin, peppercorns and vinegar in a food processor or blender and process to make a purée.

3 Place lamb in a glass or ceramic dish, spread with chilli paste, cover and marinate in the refrigerator for at least 3 hours or overnight.

4 Transfer lamb to a baking dish and roast for 3 hours or until tender. **Serves 6**

Oven temperature 150°C, 300°F, Gas 2

Slice lamb and serve with warm tortillas, vegetables and a selection of salsas.

TORTILLA PIZZA

Fresh masa can be purchased from Mexican
specialty food stores or wholesalers.

SANTA FE GRILLED BEEF

6 scotch or eye fillet steaks
1 avocado, sliced
lime wedges
2 spring onions, sliced
Spice mix
¹/₂ onion, very finely chopped
3 cloves garlic, crushed
1 tablespoon mild chilli powder
2 teaspoons grated lime rind
1 teaspoon ground cumin
2 tablespoons olive oil
1 tablespoon lime juice

1 To make spice mix, place onion, garlic, chilli powder, lime rind, cumin, oil and lime juice in a bowl and mix to combine.

2 Spread spice mix over both sides of each piece of steak and place between sheets of plastic food wrap. Pound with a meat mallet or rolling pin until steaks are 5 mm/¹/₄ in thick.

3 Cook steaks on a preheated hot barbecue or in a frying pan for 30-60 seconds each side or until tender. Serve immediately with avocado slices, lime wedges and spring onions. **Serves 6**

For a complete meal add warm tortillas, Refried Beans and a lettuce salad.

SANTA FE GRILLED BEEF

> *If you prefer the meat can be barbecued for the entire cooking time. After the initial cooking time, reduce the heat to low and cook until meat is tender. This recipe is also good made with chicken. For a complete meal, serve with warm tortillas and salad.*

PORK *with* RED CHILLI SAUCE

1 kg/2 lb boneless pork loin, trimmed of visible fat
90 g/3 oz green olives
1 onion, sliced
Rich red chilli sauce
8 ancho chillies, seeded and deveined
1 tablespoon vegetable oil
1 onion, chopped
2 cloves garlic, crushed
1 teaspoon ground cumin
1 tablespoon chopped fresh oregano
1½ cups/375mL/12 fl oz chicken or beef stock
1 cup/250 mL/8 fl oz orange juice
⅓ cup/90 mL/3 fl oz apple cider vinegar

1 To make sauce, cut chillies into flat pieces. Heat oil in a frying pan over a medium heat, add chillies and cook for a few seconds each side. Remove chillies from pan, drain on absorbent kitchen paper and place in a bowl. Pour over boiling water to cover and soak for 2-3 hours. Drain chillies and discard water.

2 Heat frying pan over a medium heat, add chopped onion and garlic and cook, stirring, for 3 minutes or until soft. Place onion mixture, chillies, cumin, oregano and ⅔ cup/170 mL/5½ fl oz stock in a food processor or blender and process to make a purée. Return mixture to frying pan and cook, stirring, for 5 minutes or mixture reduces and thickens. Stir in remaining stock, orange juice and 1 tablespoon vinegar, bring to simmering and simmer for 25 minutes or until sauce reduces and thickens. Cool.

3 Combine cool sauce with remaining vinegar. Place pork in a glass or ceramic dish and coat with one-third of the sauce, cover and marinate in the refrigerator for 2-3 hours.

4 Drain pork and cook on a preheated hot barbecue grill or in a frying pan for 2-3 minutes each side or until brown. Transfer to a baking dish and bake for 45-50 minutes or until tender. Heat remaining sauce in a saucepan over a low heat. To serve, cut pork into slices and arrange on a serving platter, spoon over sauce and scatter with olives and sliced onion. **Serves 6**

Oven temperature 150°C, 300°F, Gas 2

▶ *There is archeological evidence that certain varieties of pumpkin were grown and eaten in Mexico as long ago as 2000 BC.*

SQUASH *with* GREEN ONIONS

1 kg/2 lb butternut pumpkin peeled and chopped
350 g/11 oz yellow or green pattypan squash
4 carrots, peeled and halved
2 teaspoons finely grated lime rind
1 tablespoon olive oil
freshly ground black pepper
155 g/5 oz feta cheese, crumbled
Green onion dressing
12 spring onions, sliced
3 mild fresh green chillies, sliced
1/3 cup/90 ml/3 fl oz olive oil
1/4 cup/60 ml/2 fl oz apple cider vinegar
2 tablespoons lime juice

1 Place pumpkin, patty pan squash, carrots, lime rind, 1 tablespoon olive oil and black pepper to taste in a baking dish, toss to combine and bake for 30 minutes or until vegetables are golden and soft.

2 To make dressing, place spring onions, chillies, 1/3 cup/90 mL/3 fl oz olive oil, vinegar and lime juice in a bowl and whisk to combine.

3 Place vegetables on a serving platter, scatter with feta cheese and drizzle with dressing.

Serves 6

Oven temperature 200°C, 400°F, Gas 6

MEXICAN ORANGE SALAD

6 oranges, peeled and all white pith removed, sliced crosswise
2 red onions, sliced
90 g/3 oz toasted almonds, chopped
2 medium fresh red chillies, chopped
1/2 bunch fresh coriander (cilanto)
4 tablespoons fresh mint leaves
1/4 bunch/125 g/4 oz spinach, leaves shredded

Place oranges, onions, almonds, chillies, coriander (cilanto) leaves and mint in a bowl, toss to combine and stand for 30 minutes. Line a serving platter with spinach then pile salad on top. **Serves 6**

Garnish with extra red onion and serve with grilled meats or chicken.

ORANGE SALAD

▶ *A comal is a steel, cast iron or unglazed earthenware cooking disk, which is used for cooking and heating tortillas and for toasting other ingredients such as chillies and pumpkin seeds.*

ROASTED PEPPERS *with* HERBS

3 red capsicums (peppers)
2 green capsicums (peppers)
4 medium fresh green chillies
2 onions, quartered
2 tablespoons fresh marjoram leaves
2 tablespoons fresh thyme leaves
1/4 cup/60 ml/2 fl oz lime juice
1/4 cup/60 ml/2 fl oz olive oil

freshly ground black pepper

1 Place red and green capsicums (peppers) and chillies in a hot frying pan or comal and cook until skins are blistered and charred. Place capsicums (peppers) and chillies in a plastic food bag and stand for 10 minutes or until cool enough to handle.

2 Carefully remove skins from capsicums (peppers) and chillies, then cut off tops and remove seeds and membranes. Cut into thick slices.

3 Place onions in frying pan or comal and cook for 5 minutes or until soft and charred.

4 Place capsicums (peppers), chillies, onions, marjoram, thyme, lime juice, oil and black pepper to taste in a bowl and toss to combine. Stand for 30 minutes before serving.
Serves 6

ROASTED PEPPERS

1 Place red and green capsicums (peppers)and chillies in a hot frying pan or comal and cook until skins are blistered and charred.

2 Carefully remove skins from capsicums (peppers) and chillies, then cut off tops and remove seeds.

3 Place onions in hot frying pan or comal and cook until soft and charred.

WITH HERBS

► *Fresh epazote (chenopodium ambrosioides) is a herb much used in traditional Mexican cooking. It has an anise flavour and is often used in bean dishes as it brings out their flavour and some people believe it reduces their gaseous effects. It is not readily available commercially outside of Mexico except occasionally as a dried herb. Outside of Mexico it is called wormseed or wormweed and is often considered a weed. In Mexico dried epazote is used as a medicinal tea.*

heat until very hot, add mild chillies and cook for 2 minutes or until crisp. Drain on absorbent kitchen paper. To serve, arrange corn chips around bean mixture, then scatter with fried chilli strips. **Serves 4**

Oven temperature 180°C, 350°F, Gas 4

BLACK BEAN NACHOS

250g/8oz dried black beans, soaked overnight and drained
2¹/₂ tablespoons vegetable oil
1 onion, chopped
2 cloves garlic, crushed
2 hot fresh red chillies, chopped
1 teaspoon ground cumin
1 cup/250 mL/8 fl oz vegetable stock
125 g/4 oz grated mozzarella cheese
6 mild fresh red chillies, cut into thin strips
250 g/8 oz corn chips or fried corn tortilla pieces

1 Place beans in a saucepan and pour over fresh cold water to cover by 5 cm/2 in. Bring to the boil and boil for 10 minutes. Reduce heat, cover and simmer beans for 45 minutes or until beans are tender. Drain and set aside.

2 Heat ¹/₂ tablespoon oil in a frying pan over a medium heat, add onion, garlic, hot chillies and cumin and cook, stirring, for 3 minutes or until onions are soft. Add half the beans and cook, mashing with a potato masher until beans form a coarse purée. Add remaining beans and stock, bring to simmering and simmer for 5 minutes or until mixture reduces and thickens.

3 Transfer bean mixture to an ovenproof dish, sprinkle with cheese and bake for 20 minutes or until cheese melts.

4 Heat remaining oil in a frying pan over a high

1 Add half the beans to the frying pan and cook, mashing to form a coarse purée.

2 Transfer bean mixture to an ovenproof dish and sprinkle with cheese.

3 Cook mild chillies in hot oil for 2 minutes or until crisp.

BLACK BEAN NACHOS

These nachos are delicious served with a salsa of your choice. Shown here served with Salsa Mexicana.

POTATOES *in* CHILLI VINEGAR

2 kg/4 lb baby new potatoes, halved

CHILLI VINEGAR DRESSING
2 red onions, sliced
3 jalapeño peppers, chopped
3 fresh red chillies, seeded and chopped
2 cloves garlic, minced
2-3 tablespoons sugar
2 tablespoons capers, drained
2 tablespoons fresh thyme leaves
1 tablespoon fresh oregano leaves

4 fresh or dried bay leaves
1 cup/250 ml/8 fl oz apple cider vinegar
½ cup/125 ml/4 fl oz water

1 Place potatoes in a saucepan of boiling water and cook until tender. Drain and place in a serving bowl.

2 To make dressing, place onions, jalapeño and red chillies, garlic, sugar, capers, thyme, oregano, bay leaves, vinegar and water in a bowl and mix to combine. Pour dressing over warm potatoes, toss to combine and stand at room temperature for 2 hours before serving.

Serves 6

Don't keep this salad just for Mexican meals, it makes an interesting addition to any buffet table or salad bar. For extra zing, garnish with additional sliced chillies.

POTATOES IN CHILLI VINEGAR

Sauces and Condiments

Salsa is a word associated with Mexican food and a bowl of salsa on the side gives even the simplest meal a Mexican flavour. Salsas vary according to the cook, the season and the ingredients available, just to name a few of the changeables. A salsa can be made from raw or cooked ingredients, can be made with or without tomatoes and can be mild or hot in flavour – again it's all up to the cook, the season and ingredients available! The word salsa comes from the Spanish word for sauce and is often used instead of the word sauce. Today, most people think of a salsa as being a chunky sauce-like accompaniment.

ROASTED CHILLI SALSA

3 tomatoes
3 jalapeño or hot green chillies
1 small white onion, unpeeled
2 cloves garlic, unpeeled
1/4 teaspoon dried oregano
1/4 teaspoon ground cumin
freshly ground black pepper
water (optional)

Place tomatoes, chillies, onion and garlic in a hot dry frying pan or comal and roast until skins are blistered and charred and flesh of vegetables are soft. Peel onion and garlic, roughly chop and place in a bowl. Roughly chop tomatoes and chillies and add to onion mixture. Then add oregano, cumin and black pepper to taste. Toss to combine and thin with water, if desired.

Makes 1 1/2 cups/375 ml/12 fl oz

SALSA MEXICANA

2 ripe tomatoes, peeled, seeded
and finely chopped
2-3 hot fresh green chillies, seeded
and chopped
1 small white onion, finely chopped
1 clove garlic, minced
2 tablespoons chopped fresh coriander (cilanto)
2 tablespoons lime juice

Place tomatoes, chillies, onion, garlic, coriander (cilanto) and lime juice in a bowl and toss to combine. Stand for at least 30 minutes before serving.

Makes 2 cups/500 ml/16 fl oz

For centuries the Mexicans have enjoyed pumpkin seeds (pepitas) as a nutritious and tasty snack. In their simplest form the seeds are toasted and seasoned with salt.

PUMPKIN SEED SALSA

3 tomatoes
1 1/2 cups/45 g/1 1/2 oz green
pumpkin seeds (pepitas)
2 tablespoons water
2-3 medium fresh green chillies, chopped
2 tablespoons chopped fresh coriander (cilanto)

1 Cook tomatoes in a hot dry frying pan or comal until skins are blistered and charred. Cool slightly and peel.

2 Place pumpkin seeds (pepitas) in a baking dish and bake for 4-6 minutes or until seeds are toasted and golden. Place pumpkin seeds (pepitas) and water in a food processor or blender and process to make a rough paste. Add tomatoes, chillies and coriander (cilanto) and process to combine.

Makes 1 3/4 cups/440 ml/14 fl oz

Oven temperature 160°C, 325°F, Gas 3

ROASTED CORN SALSA

3 cobs sweet corn
1 tablespoon olive oil
1 red capsicum (pepper), quartered
3 mild fresh green chillies, halved
and seeded
2 cloves garlic, unpeeled
1 tablespoon chopped fresh coriander (cilanto)
2 teaspoons chopped fresh oregano

1 Brush corn cobs with oil and cook on a preheated hot char-grill or barbecue for 6-8 minutes or until lightly charred and soft. Cut corn from cobs and place in a bowl.

2 Brush red capsicum and chillies with oil and cook on preheated hot char-grill or barbecue with garlic for 4 minutes or until skins are

lightly charred. Chop red pepper and chillies and squeeze garlic from skins. Add red pepper, chillies, garlic, coriander and oregano to sweet corn and toss to combine.

Makes 2 cups/500 ml/16 fl oz

SALSA VERDE

500 g/1 lb canned tomatillos, drained
and roughly chopped
2-3 medium fresh green chillies, seeded
and chopped
1 small white onion, chopped
1 clove garlic, chopped
2 tablespoons fresh coriander (cilanto) leaves
pinch ground cumin

Place tomatillos, chillies, onion, garlic, coriander (cilanto) and cumin in a food processor and process to finely chopped. Chill.

Makes 1¹/₂ cups/375 ml/12 fl oz

This green salsa is even better if made with fresh tomatillos instead of the canned ones.

SALSA RANCHERA

2 teaspoons vegetable oil
1 green capsicum (pepper), chopped
1 onion, chopped
2 medium fresh green chillies,
seeded and chopped
2 cloves garlic, chopped
5 ripe tomatoes, roasted, peeled, seeded
and chopped
1 tablespoon chopped fresh oregano
1 teaspoon ground cumin
1 tablespoon chopped fresh coriander

Heat oil in a frying pan over a medium heat, add green capsicum, onion, chillies and garlic and cook, stirring, for 4 minutes or until vegetables are soft. Add tomatoes, oregano and cumin and simmer for 10 minutes or until sauce reduces and thickens. Stir in coriander (cilanto).

Makes 2 cups/500 ml/16 fl oz

This standard salsa is great served with grilled meats, chicken and fish. It is also the base sauce for the well known huevos rancheros – once the sauce is cooked make four indentations in the sauce, break in 4 eggs, and cook for 5 minutes longer or until eggs are cooked to your liking.

GARLIC *and* CHILLI SALSA

4 medium fresh green chillies, seeded
and chopped
2 tomatoes, peeled and chopped
6 cloves garlic, chopped
1 tablespoon chopped fresh coriander (cilanto)
2 tablespoons chopped fresh flat
leaf parsley
1 teaspoon ground cumin
2 teaspoons lime juice

Place chillies, tomatoes, garlic, coriander (cilanto), parsley and cumin in a food processor or blender and process to roughly chopped. Stir in lime juice and chill until required.

Makes 1 cup/250 ml/8 fl oz

ENCHILADA SAUCE

500 g/1 lb canned tomatillos, drained and chopped
1 white onion, chopped
1 hot fresh green chilli, seeded
and chopped
1 clove garlic, minced
2 tablespoons fresh coriander (cilanto) leaves
1 cup/250 ml/8 fl oz chicken or vegetable stock
lime juice

Place tomatillos, onion, chilli, garlic and coriander (cilanto) in a food processor or blender and process until smooth. Transfer to a saucepan and bring to simmering over a low heat. Stir in stock and simmer for 8-10 minutes or until sauce reduces and thickens. Stir in lime juice to taste. **Makes 13/4 cups/440 ml/14 fl oz**

Tomatillos look like green tomatoes but they aren't – in fact they don't even belong to the same family. They are also known as cape gooseberries and ground cherries.

Glossary

Fresh Chillies

Habanero: The habanero chilli is closely related to the Scotch Bonnet chilli for which it is sometimes mistaken. The habanero is the hottest chilli in the world and the Scotch Bonnet is only slightly less hot. Both are small lantern-shaped chillies, the habanero is about 5 cm/2 in long and the Scotch Bonnet is just a little smaller. Habaneros are said to be 30-50 times hotter than jalapeños. The habanero is also available dried and smoked dried. When dried it is mostly used for sauces and as with the fresh should be used with caution.

Jalapeño: Available as red or green this is one of the most popular and best known chillies. Being the riper form the red jalapeño chilli is sweeter than the green.

Poblano: The colour of this cone-shaped chilli ranges from green to red. It is one of the most popular chillies used in Mexican cooking, is used at all stages of ripeness and is seldom eaten raw. Poblano chillies are most often roasted and stuffed, used in moles and sauces or as roasted chilli strips. If poblano chillies are unavailable one of the other mild chillies such as Anaheim or New Mexico could be used instead.

Serrano: This green or red chilli is considered by many to be the best one for salsas. Serrano literally means 'from the mountains' and it was in the mountains of northern Puebla and Hidalgo in Mexico that this chilli was first grown. If unavailable use jalapeño chillies instead. In Mexico serrano and jalapeño chillies are considered to be interchangable.

Dried Chillies

Ancho: This chilli is the dried form of the poblano chilli and is the most popular dried chilli in Mexico. It is the sweetest of the dried chillies and adds a sweet-smoky flavour to dishes. It is much used in moles and other sauces.

Chipotle: This is a dried, smoked jalapeño chilli which adds a smoky hot flavour to dishes. They are also available canned usually in an adobo sauce which takes up the flavour of the chilli.

Guajillo: This mild to medium chilli has a piney, slightly fruity flavour and is mostly used in salsas, sauces, soups and stews.

Pasilla: This chilli is also known as chilli negro. The name pasilla means 'little raisin' and this chilli has a raisin-like aroma with a wrinkled raisin-coloured skin.
Along with the ancho and mulato chillies it one of the three chillies known as the 'holy trinity' which are used in the preparation of mole nero (black).

Banana leaves: Like corn husks these are used for wrapping food and impart a distinctive flavour. They are never eaten. Before using for wrapping fresh leaves need to softened. This can be done by: passing the leaves over a gas flame until they are soft; blanching in boiling water for 20-30 seconds; or heating in the microwave on HIGH (100%) for 45-60 seconds or until soft. Remove the thick mid-rib before using or the leaves will be difficult to wrap around the food. Banana leaves are used more often in southern and coastal Mexico.

Comal: This is a cooking disk made from steel, cast iron or unglazed earthenware and is traditionally used for cooking tortillas. It is also used for roasting or toasting ingredients such as pumpkin seeds and chillies and is an essential piece of equipment for any Mexican cook. A heavy skillet or frying pan are suitable alternatives.

Glossary

Corn husks: These are the dried outer leaves of the corn husks which are used for wrapping tamales and various other foods. They need to be soaked well before using so that they become soft and pliable and are easier to wrap around the food. They are available from specialty food stores.

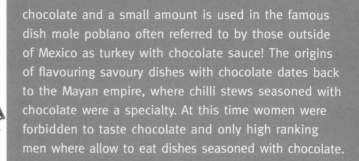

Masa: In Mexico masa refers to corn dough which is used for making tortillas. Fresh masa is available from specialty Mexican food stores or can sometimes be purchased from good Mexican restaurants. If it is unavailable make your own using masa harina (for more information see below). The flavour of tortillas made with masa harina will be slightly different to those made with fresh masa but for many it will be an easier and more convenient alternative. Instant masa is sometimes available – follow packet directions for how to use.

Masa harina: This flour-like powder is fresh corn masa which has been dried and finely ground. It should not be confused with corn meal (polenta) which cannot be used for making tortillas. If you are unable to obtain fresh masa, then use masa harina. To reconstitute masa harina it is usually simply a matter adding water and sometimes butter or some other fat, however for best results follow the packet directions. Masa harina is available from stores specialising in Mexican food stuffs.

Mexican chocolate: This does not resemble European chocolate in the slightest. Rather than being velvety and smooth it is grainy and is never eaten as confectionery. Mexican chocolate is made by grinding together cacao beans, sugar, canela (Mexican soft cinnamon) and almonds, then pressing the mixture into tablets. It is primarily used for making hot chocolate and a small amount is used in the famous dish mole poblano often referred to by those outside of Mexico as turkey with chocolate sauce! The origins of flavouring savoury dishes with chocolate dates back to the Mayan empire, where chilli stews seasoned with chocolate were a specialty. At this time women were forbidden to taste chocolate and only high ranking men where allow to eat dishes seasoned with chocolate.

Pumpkin seeds: For centuries the Mexicans have enjoyed pumpkin seeds as a nutritious and tasty snack. In their simplest form the seeds are toasted and seasoned with salt. Often called pepitas, they are simply the dried seeds of pumpkin and various other squash. In Mexico pumpkin seeds can be purchased raw, roasted, shelled, unshelled or ground. Pumpkin seed sauce is a popular accompaniment for simply prepared meat, poultry, fish and vegetables or can be offered as dip for tortillas.

Tomatillos: While these look like green tomatoes, and are often called Mexican green tomatoes, they don't even belong to the tomato family. Instead they are a member of the gooseberry family and can also be called cape gooseberries and ground cherries. Tomatillos can be difficult to buy fresh outside of Mexico, however they are readily available canned and these make a good alternative if fresh are unavailable and means that no cooking is required.

Tortilla press: These are available from specialty Mexican food stores or kitchenware shops and make the process of shaping tortillas a little quicker and easier. The best tortilla presses are made from cast iron or wood.

Index

Aztec Flower Soup	37
Barbecue Chilli Prawns	48
Barbecued Squid Salad	9
Beef Tostada Cups	38
Beef with Peppercorns	11
Black Bean Nachos	70
Cardamom and Orange Duck	20
Cashew and Chilli Beef Curry	24
Cellophane Noodle Salad	36
Charcoal-Grilled Chicken	32
Cheese and Bean Quesadillas	44
Chicken and Chilli Tamales	43
Chicken in Banana Leaves	59
Chicken in Pumpkin Seed Sauce	60
Chicken Phanaeng Curry	26
Chicken Tortillas	44
Chicken with Chilli Jam	10
Chicken with Garlic and Pepper	32
Chicken with Lime and Coconut	26
Chilli Fried Rice	35
Chilli Kumara Soup	7
Coconut Prawns and Scallops	12
Contents	4
Crispy Lamb Tortilla Pizza	62
Deep-Fried Chilli Fish	28
Eggplant and Basil Stir-Fry	17
Enchilada Sauce	74
Feta-Stuffed Ancho Chillies	38
Fish Baked in Corn Husks	50
Fish Cakes with Relish	5
Fish with Green Mango Sauce	28
Fish with Lime and Garlic	31
Fish with Marinated Onions	56
Flavours of Mexico	37
Garlic and Chilli Salsa	74
Glossary	75
Green Chilli and Prawn Curry	23
Grilled Scallops with Salsa	53
Hot and Sour Seafood Soup	6
Marinated Lime Fish	56
Mexican Orange Salad	66
Minted Bean Curry	22
Mussels with Coconut Vinegar	19
New Mexico Enchiladas	39
Pad Thai	34
Pinto Bean Soup	47
Pork and Majoram Taquitos	42
Pork and Pumpkin Stir-Fry	14
Pork with Garlic and Pepper	14
Pork with Red Chilli Sauce	65
Potatoes in Chilli Vinegar	72
Prawn Empanadas	46
Prawn Tostaditas	48
Pumpkin Seed Salsa	73
Red Beef Curry	24
Rice Cakes with Lime Crab	4
Roasted Chilli Duck	61
Roasted Chilli Salsa	73
Roasted Corn Salsa	73
Roasted Garlic Fish	52
Roasted Peppers with Herbs	68
Salsa Mexicana	73
Salsa Ranchera	74
Salsa Verde	74
Santa Fe Grilled Beef	64
Seafood Tacos	53
Shellfish with Lemon Grass	30
Skewers with Tomato Sauce	54
Slow-Baked Chilli Lamb	62
Spiced Mussels in Vinegar	55
Spiced Shredded Beef	58
Squash with Lemon Greens	66
Stir-Fried Bitter Melon	16
Stir-Fried Duck with Greens	13
Stir-Fried Tararind Prawns	18
Stuffed Poblano Chillies	40
Tastes of Thailand	4
Thai Beef Salad	8
That Green Curry	21

Cooking Notes